THE PLOU
THE S

A Tragedy in Four Acts

by
SEAN O'CASEY

Samuel French - London
New York - Toronto - Hollywood

822.912
O15p

THE PLOUGH AND THE STARS

Produced at the Fortune Theatre, London, on the 12th May 1926, with the following cast of characters—

JACK CLITHEROE, a bricklayer—Commandant in the Irish Citizen Army		David Marris
NORA CLITHEROE, his wife		Eileen Carey
PETER FLYNN, a labourer—Nora's uncle		J. A. O'Rourke
THE YOUNG COVEY, a fitter—Clitheroe's cousin	Residents	Sydney Morgan
BESSIE BURGESS, a street fruit-vendor	in the	Sara Allgood
MRS GOGAN, a charwoman	Tenement	Marie O'Neill
MOLLSER, her consumptive child		Joyce Chancellor
FLUTHER GOOD, a carpenter		Arthur Sinclair
LIEUT. LANGON, a Civil Servant—of the Irish Volunteers		Harry Hutchinson
CAPT. BRENNAN, a chicken butcher—of the Irish Citizen Army		Felix Irwin
CORPORAL STODDART, of the Wiltshires		Edwin Ellis
SERGEANT TINLEY, of the Wiltshires		Christopher Steele
ROSIE REDMOND, a daughter of 'the Digs'		Kathleen Drago
A BAR-TENDER		E. J. Kennedy
A WOMAN		No Woman
THE FIGURE IN THE WINDOW		Barney Mulligan

SYNOPSIS OF SCENES

ACT I

The Living-room of the Clitheroe flat in a Dublin tenement

ACT II

A Public-house, outside of which a meeting is being held

ACT III

The Street outside the Clitheroe tenement

ACT IV

The Room of Bessie Burgess

*Time. Acts I and II, November 1915; Acts III and IV, Easter Week, 1916.
A few days elapse between Acts III and IV*

THE PLOUGH AND THE STARS

ACT I

SCENE—*The Home of the Clitheroes. It consists of the front and back drawing-rooms in a fine old Georgian house, struggling for its life against the assaults of time, and the more savage assaults of the tenants. The room shown is the back drawing-room, wide, spacious and lofty. At back is the entrance to the front drawing-room. The space, originally occupied by folding doors, is now draped with casement cloth of a dark purple, decorated with a design in reddish-purple. One of the curtains is pulled aside, giving a glimpse of the front drawing-room, at the end of which can be seen the wide, lofty windows looking out into the street. The room directly in front of the audience is furnished in a way that suggests an attempt towards a finer expression of domestic life. The large fireplace on L is of wood, painted to look like marble (the original has been taken away by the landlord). Below the fireplace, on the wall, is a small mirror. On the mantelshelf are two candlesticks of dark carved wood. Between them is a small clock. Over the clock, on wall, is a picture of 'The Sleeping Venus'. On the right of the entrance to the front drawing-room is a copy of 'The Gleaners', on the opposite side a copy of 'The Angelus'. Underneath 'The Gleaners' is a chest of drawers on which stands a green bowl filled with scarlet dahlias and white chrysanthemums. Near to the fireplace is a couch which at night forms a double bed for Clitheroe and Nora. Near the end of the room opposite to the fireplace is a gate-legged table, covered with a cloth. On top of the table a huge cavalry sword is lying. To the L above the fireplace is a door which leads to a lobby from which the staircase leads to the hall. The floor is covered with a dark green linoleum. The room is dim except where it is illuminated from the glow of the fire.*

When the CURTAIN *rises,* FLUTHER GOOD *is repairing the lock of the door,* L. *A claw hammer is on a chair beside him, and he has a screwdriver in his hand. He is a man of forty years of age, rarely surrendering to thoughts of anxiety, fond of his 'oil' but determined to conquer the habit before he dies. He is square-jawed and harshly featured ; under the left eye is a scar, and his nose is bent from a smashing blow received in a fistic battle long ago. He is bald, save for a few peeping tufts of reddish hair around his ears ; and his upper lip is hidden by a scrubby red moustache, embroidered here and there with a grey hair. He is dressed in a seedy black suit, cotton shirt with a soft collar, and wears a very respectable little black bow. On his head is a faded jerry*

1

hat, which, when he is excited, he has a habit of knocking farther back on his head, in a series of taps. In an argument he usually fills with sound and fury, generally signifying a row. He is in his shirt sleeves at present, and wears a soiled white apron, from a pocket in which sticks a carpenter's two-foot rule. He has just finished the job of putting on a new lock, and, filled with satisfaction, he is opening and shutting the door, enjoying the completion of a work well done. Sitting at the fire, airing a white shirt, is Peter Flynn. *He is a little, thin bit of a man, with a face shaped like a lozenge; on his cheeks and under his chin is a straggling wiry beard of a dirty-white and lemon hue. His face invariably wears a look of animated anguish, mixed with irritated defiance, as if everybody was at war with him, and he at war with everybody. He is cocking his head in such a way that suggests resentment at the presence of* Fluther, *who pays no attention to him, apparently, but is really furtively watching him.* Peter *is clad in a singlet, white whipcord knee-breeches, and is in his stockinged feet.*

A voice is heard speaking outside of the door L (*it is that of* Mrs Gogan *talking to someone*).

Mrs Gogan (*outside the door* L) Who are you lookin' for, sir? Who? Mrs Clitheroe? . . . Oh, excuse me. Oh ay, up this way. She's out, I think: I seen her goin'. Oh, you've somethin' for her. Oh, excuse me. You're from Arnott's . . . I see . . . You've a parcel for her . . . Righto . . . I'll take it . . . I'll give it to her the minute she comes in . . . It'll be quite safe . . . Oh, sign that . . . Excuse me . . . Where? . . . Here? . . . No, there; righto. Am I to put Maggie or Mrs? What is it? You dunno? Oh, excuse me.

Mrs Gogan *opens the door and comes in. She is a doleful-looking little woman of forty, with an insinuating manner and sallow complexion. She is fidgety and nervous, terribly talkative, has a habit of taking up things that may be near her and fiddling with them while she is speaking. Her heart is aflame with curiosity, and a fly could not come into nor go out of the house without her knowing. She has a draper's parcel in her hand; the knot of the twine tying it is untied.* Mrs Gogan *crosses in front of Fluther, behind the couch, to the table* R, *where she puts the parcel, fingering it till she has the paper off, showing a cardboard box.* Peter, *more resentful of this intrusion than of Fluther's presence, gets up from the chair, and without looking around, his head carried at an angry cock, marches into the room at the back. He leaves the shirt on the back of the chair.*

(*Removing the paper and opening the cardboard box it contains*) I wondher what's this now? A hat! (*She takes out a hat, black, with decorations in red and gold*) God, she's goin' to th' divil lately for style! That hat, now, cost more than a penny. Such notions of upperosity she's getting. (*She puts the hat on her head*) Swank! (*Turning to Fluther*) Eh, Fluther, swank, what!

(FLUTHER *looks over at her, then goes on opening and shutting the door*)

FLUTHER. She's a pretty little Judy, all the same.

MRS GOGAN. Ah, she is, an' she isn't. There's prettiness an' prettiness in it. I'm always sayin' that her skirts are a little too short for a married woman. An' to see her, sometimes of an evenin', in her glad-neck gown would make a body's blood run cold. I do be ashamed of me life before her husband. An' th' way she thries to be polite, with her 'Good mornin', Mrs Gogan,' when she's goin' down, an' her 'Good evenin', Mrs Gogan,' when she's comin' up. But there's politeness an' politeness in it.

FLUTHER. They seem to get on well together, all th' same.

MRS GOGAN. Ah, they do, an' they don't. The pair o' them used to be like two turtle doves always billin' an' cooin'. You couldn't come into th' room but you'd feel, instinctive like, that they'd just been after kissin' an' cuddlin' each other . . . It often made me shiver, for, after all, there's kissin' an' cuddlin' in it. But I'm thinkin' he's beginnin' to take things more quietly; the mystery of havin' a woman's a mystery no longer . . . She dhresses herself to keep him with her, but it's no use—afther a month or two, th' wondher of a woman wears off.

(MRS GOGAN *takes off the hat, and puts it back in the box; she goes on to rearrange paper round the box, and tie it up again*)

FLUTHER. I dunno, I dunno. Not wishin' to say anything derogatory, I think it's all a question of location: when a man finds th' wondher of one woman beginnin' to die, it's usually beginnin' to live in another.

MRS GOGAN. She's always grumblin' about havin' to live in a tenement house. 'I wouldn't like to spend me last hour in one, let alone live me life in a tenement,' says she. 'Vaults,' says she, 'that are hidin' th' dead, instead of homes that are sheltherin' th' livin'.' 'Many a good one,' says I, 'was reared in a tenement house.' Oh, you know, she's a well-up little lassie, too; able to make a shillin' go where another would have to spend a pound. She's wipin' th' eyes of th' Covey an' poor oul' Pether—everybody knows that—screwin' every penny she can out o' them, in ordher to turn th' place into a babby-house. An' she has th' life frightened out o' them; washin' their face, combin' their hair, wipin' their feet, brushin' their clothes, thrimmin' their nails, cleanin' their teeth—God Almighty, you'd think th' poor men were undhergoin' penal servitude.

FLUTHER (*with an exclamation of disgust*) A-a-ah, that's goin' beyond th' beyonds in a tenement house. That's a little bit too derogatory.

(PETER *enters from the room, back, head elevated and resentful fire in his eyes; he is still in his singlet and trousers, but is now wearing a pair of unlaced boots—possibly to be decent in the presence of Mrs Gogan. He comes down c and crosses, in front of the settee, to the chair in front of the fire; he turns the shirt which he has left to air on the back of the chair, then goes, in front of the couch, to the chest of drawers, back L, and opens drawer after drawer, looking for something; as he fails to find it, he closes each drawer with a snap. He jerks out things neatly folded, and shoves them back into the drawers any way)*

PETER *(in anguish, snapping a drawer shut)* Well, God Almighty give me patience.

(PETER returns, in front of the couch, to the fireplace, gives the shirt a vicious turn on the back of the chair, and goes back, in front of the couch, to the room, back, FLUTHER and MRS GOGAN watching him furtively all the time)

MRS GOGAN *(curiously)* I wondher what is he foostherin' for now?

FLUTHER *(coming c)* He's adornin' himself for the meeting tonight. *(He pulls a handbill from one of his pockets, and reads)* 'Great Demonsthration an' Torchlight Procession around places in the City sacred to th' memory of Irish Pathriots to be concluded be a meetin', at which will be taken an oath of fealty to th' Irish Republic. Formation in Parnell Square at eight o'clock.' Well, they can hold it for Fluther. I'm up th' pole; no more dhrink for Fluther. It's three days now since I touched a dhrop, an' I feel a new man already. *(He goes back to the door L)*

MRS GOGAN. Isn't oul' Peter a funny-lookin' little man? . . . Like somethin' you'd pick off a Christmas Tree . . . When he's dhressed up in his canonicals, you'd wondher where he'd been got. God forgive me, when I see him in them, I always think he must ha' had a Mormon for a father! He an' th' Covey can't abide each other; th' pair o' them is always at it, thryin' to best each other. There'll be blood dhrawn one o' these days.

FLUTHER. How is it that Clitheroe himself, now, doesn't have anythin' to do with th' Citizen Army? A couple o' months ago, an' you'd hardly ever see him without his gun, an' th' Red Hand o' Liberty Hall in his hat.

MRS GOGAN. Just because he wasn't made a Captain of. He wasn't goin' to be in anything where he couldn't be conspishuous. He was so cocksure o' being made one that he bought a Sam Browne belt, an' was always puttin' it on an' standin' at th' door showing it off, till th' man came an' put out th' street lamps on him. God, I think he used to bring it to bed with him! But I'm tellin' you herself was delighted that that cock didn't crow, for she's like a clockin' hen if he leaves her sight for a minute. *(While she is talking she takes up a book from the table, looks into it in a near-sighted way, and then leaves it back. She now lifts up the sword, and proceeds to examine it)* Be th' look of it, this must ha' been a general's sword . . . All th' gold lace an' th' fine figaries on it . . . Sure it's twiced too big for him.

(FLUTHER *crosses from the door* L *behind the couch, back of the table, where* MRS GOGAN *is examining the sword, and looks at it, standing to* L *of Mrs Gogan*)

FLUTHER (*contemptuously*) Ah, it's a baby's rattle he ought to have, an' he as he is, with thoughts tossin' in his head of what may happen to him on th' Day of Judgement.

(PETER *appears at the curtained door, back, sees Mrs Gogan with the sword, and a look of vexation comes on to his face. He comes down* C *to the table, snatches the sword out of Mrs Gogan's hands, and bangs it back on the table. He then returns into the room, back, without speaking*)

MRS GOGAN (*to Peter, as he snatches the sword*) Oh, excuse me. (*To Fluther*) Isn't he the surly oul' rascal, Fluther? (*She wanders from the table, back of the couch, to the chest of drawers, where she stops for a few moments, pulling out drawers and pushing them in again*)

FLUTHER (*leaning against the left side of the table*) Take no notice of him . . . You'd think he was dumb, but when you get his goat, or he has a few jars up, he's vice versa.

(FLUTHER *coughs.* MRS GOGAN, *who has wandered from the chest of drawers, down* L, *to the fireplace, where she is fingering Peter's shirt, turns to look at Fluther, as soon as she hears the cough*)

MRS GOGAN (*with an ominous note in her voice*) Oh, you've got a cold on you, Fluther.

FLUTHER (*carelessly*) Ah, it's only a little one.

MRS GOGAN. You'd want to be careful, all th' same. I knew a woman, a big lump of a woman, red-faced an' round-bodied, a little awkward on her feet; you'd think, to look at her, she could put out her two arms an' lift a two-storied house on th' top of her head; got a ticklin' in her throat, an' a little cough, an' th' next mornin' she had a little catchin' in her chest, an' they had just time to wet her lips with a little rum, an' off she went. (*She begins to look at and handle the shirt*)

FLUTHER (*a little nervously*) It's only a little cold I have; there's nothing derogatory wrong with me.

MRS GOGAN (*warningly*) I dunno; there's many a man this minute lowerin' a pint, thinkin' of a woman, or pickin' out a winner, or doin' work as you're doin', while th' hearse dhrawn be th' horses with the black plumes is dhrivin' up to his own hall door, an' a voice that he doesn't hear is muttherin' in his ear, 'Earth to earth, an' ashes t' ashes, an' dust to dust.'

FLUTHER (*faintly, affected by her talk*) A man in th' pink o' health should have a holy horror of allowin' thoughts o' death to be festherin' in his mind, for (*with a frightened cough*) be God, I think

I'm afther gettin' a little catch in me chest that time—it's a creepy thing to be thinkin' about.

(FLUTHER *sits weakly in the chair* L *of the table*)

MRS GOGAN. It is, an' it isn't; it's both bad an' good . . . It always gives meself a kind o' thresspassin' joy to feel meself movin' along in a mournin' coach, an' me thinkin' that, maybe, th' next funeral 'll be me own, an' glad, in a quiet way, that this is somebody else's.

FLUTHER (*very frightened*) An' a curious kind of gaspin' for breath—I hope there's nothin' derogatory wrong with me.

MRS GOGAN (*examining the shirt*) Frills on it, like a woman's petticoat.

FLUTHER (*panic-stricken*) Suddenly gettin' hot, an' then, just as suddenly, gettin' cold.

MRS GOGAN (*holding out the shirt towards Fluther*) How would you like to be wearin' this Lord Mayor's nightdhress, Fluther?

FLUTHER (*vehemently*) Blast you an' your nightshirt! Is a man fermentin' with fear to stick th' showin' off to him of a thing that looks like a shinin' shroud?

MRS GOGAN (*startled at Fluther's vehemence*) Oh, excuse me.

(PETER *appears at the curtained door, back. He sees his shirt in Mrs Gogan's hand, comes rapidly down* C, *goes in front of the couch to Mrs Gogan, snatches the shirt from her, and replaces it on the back of the chair; he returns the same way to the room, back*)

PETER (*loudly, as he goes to the room, back*) Well, God Almighty give me patience!

MRS GOGAN (*to Peter*) Oh, excuse me.

(*There is heard a cheer from the men working outside on the street, followed by the clang of tools being thrown down, then silence*)

(*Running into the back room to look out of the window*) What's the men repairin' th' streets cheerin' for?

FLUTHER (*sitting down weakly on a chair*) You can't sneeze but that oul' one wants to know th' why an' th' wherefore . . . I feel as dizzy as bedamned! I hope I didn't give up th' beer too suddenly.

(*The* COVEY *comes in by the door* L. *He is about twenty-five, tall, thin, with lines on his face that form a perpetual protest against life as he conceives it to be. Heavy seams fall from each side of his nose, down around his lips, as if they were suspenders keeping his mouth from falling. He speaks in a slow, wailing drawl; more rapidly when he is excited. He is dressed in dungarees, and is wearing a vividly red tie. He comes down* C *and flings his cap with a gesture of disgust on the table, and begins to take off his overalls*)

MRS GOGAN (*to the Covey, as she runs back into the room*) What's after happenin', Covey?

THE COVEY (*with contempt*) Th' job's stopped. They've been mobilized to march in th' demonstration tonight undher th' Plough an' th' Stars.. Didn't you hear them cheerin', th' mugs. They have to renew their political baptismal vows to be faithful in *seculo seculorum*.

FLUTHER (*sitting on the chair* L *of the table, forgetting his fear in his indignation*) There's no reason to bring religion into it. I think we ought to have as great a regard for religion as we can, so as to keep it out of as many things as possible.

THE COVEY (*pausing in the taking off of his dungarees*) Oh, you're one o' the boys that climb into religion as high as a short Mass on Sunday mornin's? I suppose you'll be singin' songs o' Sion an' songs o' Tara at th' meetin', too.

FLUTHER. We're all Irishmen, anyhow; aren't we?

THE COVEY (*with hand outstretched, and in a professorial tone*) Look here, comrade, there's no such thing as an Irishman, or an Englishman, or a German or a Turk; we're all only human bein's. Scientifically speakin', it's all a question of the accidental gatherin' together of mollycewels an' atoms.

(PETER *comes in from the room, back, with a stiff collar in his hand, comes down* C, *crosses, in front of the couch, to the mirror on the wall* L, *below the fireplace. He stands before the mirror and tries to put on his collar.* FLUTHER *gets up from the chair, goes* C *and stands to* R *of the Covey*)

FLUTHER. Mollycewels an' atoms! d'ye think I'm goin' to listen to you thryin' to juggle Fluther's mind with complicated cunundhrums of mollycewels an' atoms?

THE COVEY (*rather loudly*) There's nothin' complicated in it. There's no fear o' th' Church tellin' you that mollycewels is a stickin' together of millions of atoms o' sodium, carbon, potassium o' iodide, etcetera, that, accordin' to th' way they're mixed, make a flower, a fish, a star that you see shinin' in th' sky, or a man with a big brain like me, or a man with a little brain like you!

FLUTHER (*more loudly still*) There's no necessity to be raisin' your voice; shoutin's no manifestin' forth of a growin' mind.

(FLUTHER *and the* COVEY *turn to look at Peter*)

PETER (*struggling with his collar*) God give me patience with this thing . . . She makes these collars as stiff with starch as a shinin' band of solid steel! She does it purposely to thry an twart me. If I can't get it on to the singlet, how in the name of God am I goin' to get it on the shirt!

(FLUTHER *and the* COVEY *face each other again*)

THE COVEY (*loudly*) There's no use o' arguin' with you; it's education you want, comrade.

FLUTHER (*sarcastically*) The Covey an' God made th' world I suppose, wha'?

THE COVEY (*jeering*) When I hear some men talkin' I'm inclined to disbelieve that the world's eight-hundhred million years old, for it's not long since th' fathers o' some o' them crawled out o' th' sheltherin' slime o' the sea.

MRS GOGAN (*from the room at back*) There, they're afther formin' fours, an' now they're goin' to march away.

FLUTHER (*scornfully taking no notice of Mrs Gogan*) Mollycewels! (*He begins to untie his apron*) What about Adam an' Eve?

THE COVEY. Well, what about them?

FLUTHER (*fiercely*) What about them, you?

THE COVEY. Adam an' Eve! Is that as far as you've got? Are you still thinkin' there was nobody in th' world before Adam an' Eve? (*Loudly*) Did you ever hear, man, of th' skeleton of th' man o' Java?

PETER (*casting the collar from him*) Blast it, blast it, blast it! (*He angrily picks up the collar he has thrown on the floor, goes up* C, *right of the couch, to the chest of drawers, and begins to hunt again in the drawers*)

FLUTHER (*to the Covey, as he viciously folds his apron*) Ah, you're not goin' to be let tap your rubbidge o' thoughts into th' mind o' Fluther.

THE COVEY. You're afraid to listen to th' truth!

FLUTHER (*pugnaciously*) Who's afraid?

THE COVEY. You are!

FLUTHER (*with great contempt*) G'way, you wurum!

THE COVEY. Who's a worum?

FLUTHER. You are, or you wouldn't talk th' way you're talkin'.

(MRS GOGAN *wanders in from the room, back, turns* L, *sees Peter at the chest of drawers, turns back, comes down* C, *goes, in front of the couch, to the fireplace*)

THE COVEY. Th' oul', ignorant savage leppin' up in you, when science shows you that th' head of your god is an empty one. Well, I hope you're enjoyin' th' blessin' o' havin' to live be th' sweat of your brow.

FLUTHER. You'll be kickin' an' yellin' for th' priest yet, me boyo. I'm not goin' to stand silent an' simple listenin' to a thick like you makin' a maddenin' mockery o' God Almighty. It 'ud be a nice derogatory thing on me conscience, an' me dyin', to look back in rememberin' shame of talkin' to a word-weavin' little ignorant yahoo of a red flat Socialist!

MRS GOGAN (*at the fireplace, turning to look at the disputants*) For God's sake, Fluther, dhrop it; there's always th' makin's of a row in the mention of religion. (*She turns her head, and looks at the picture of 'The Sleeping Venus', hanging over the mantelpiece. She looks at it intently and a look of astonishment comes on her face)* God bless us, it's the picture of a naked woman. *(With a titter)* Look, Fluther.

(FLUTHER looks over at the fireplace; comes slowly to the fireplace; looks steadily at the picture. PETER, hearing what was said, leaves the chest of drawers, and comes down, standing a little behind Fluther and Mrs Gogan, and looks at the picture. The COVEY looks on from c)

FLUTHER. What's undher it? *(Reading slowly)* 'Georgina: The Sleeping Vennis.' Oh, that's a terrible picture . . . Oh, that's a shockin' picture! *(Peering into it with evident pleasure)* Oh, the one that got that taken, she must ha' been a prime lassie!

PETER *(laughing in a silly way, with head tilted back)* Hee, hee, hee, hee, hee!

FLUTHER *(indignantly, to Peter)* What are you hee, hee-in' for? *(Pointing to the picture)* That's a nice thing to be hee, hee-in' at. Where's your morality, man?

MRS GOGAN *(looking intently at it)* God forgive us, it's not right to be lookin' at it.

FLUTHER. It's nearly a derogatory thing to be in th' room where it is.

MRS GOGAN *(giggling hysterically)* I couldn't stop any longer in th' same room with three men, afther lookin' at it!

(MRS GOGAN goes up stage L, and out by the door L. The COVEY, who has taken off his dungarees, seeing Peter's shirt on the chair, throws his dungarees over it with a contemptuous movement)

PETER *(roused by the Covey's action)* Where are you throwin' your dungarees? Are you thryin' to twart an' torment me again?

THE COVEY. Who's thryin' to twart you?

(PETER takes the dungarees from the back of the chair and flings them violently on the floor)

PETER. You're not goin' to make me lose me temper, me young covey!

(The COVEY, in retaliation, takes Peter's white shirt from the back of the chair, and flings it violently on the floor)

THE COVEY. If you're Nora's pet aself, you're not goin' to get your own way in everything.

(The COVEY moves to the back end of the table, enjoying Peter's anger)

PETER *(plaintively, with his eyes looking up at the ceiling)* I'll say nothin' . . . I'll leave you to th' day when th' all-pitiful, all-merciful, all-lovin' God'll be handin' you to th' angels to be rievin' an' roastin' you, tearin' an' tormentin' you, burnin' an' blastin' you!

THE COVEY. Aren't you th' little malignant oul' bastard, you lemon-whiskered oul' swine!

(PETER *rushes to the table, takes up the sword, draws it from its scabbard, and makes for the* COVEY, *who runs round the table* R, *followed by* PETER)

(*Dodging round the table, to Fluther*) Fluther, hold him there. It's a nice thing to have a lunatic, like this, lashing round with a lethal weapon!

(*The* COVEY, *after running round the table, rushes up* C, *and runs back of the couch, out of the door* L, *which he bangs to behind him in the face of Peter.* FLUTHER *remains near the fireplace, looking on*)

PETER (*hammering at the door, to the Covey, outside*) Lemme out, lemme out. Isn't it a poor thing for a man who wouldn't say a word against his greatest enemy to have to listen to that Covey's twartin' animosities, shovin' poor, patient people into a lashin' out of curses that darken his soul with th' shadow of th' wrath of th' last day!

FLUTHER. Why d'ye take notice of him? If he seen you didn't, he'd say nothin' derogatory.

PETER. I'll make him stop his laughin' an' leerin', jibin' an' jeerin' an' scarifyin' people with his corner-boy insinuations! . . . He's always thryin' to rouse me: if it's not a song, it's a whistle; if it isn't a whistle, it's a cough. But you can taunt an' taunt— I'm laughin' at you; he, hee, hee, hee, hee, heee!

THE COVEY (*jeering loudly through the keyhole*) Dear harp o' me counthry, in darkness I found thee,
The dark chain of silence had hung o'er thee long——

PETER (*frantically to Fluther*) Jasus, d'ye hear that? D'ye hear him soundin' forth his divil-souled song o' provocation? (*Battering at the door* L) When I get out I'll do for you, I'll do for you, I'll do for you!

THE COVEY (*through the keyhole*) Cuckoo-oo!

(NORA *enters by the door* L. *She is a young woman of twenty-three, alert, swift, full of nervous energy, and a little anxious to get on in the world. The firm lines of her face are considerably opposed by a soft, amorous mouth, and gentle eyes. When her firmness fails her, she persuades with her feminine charm. She is dressed in a tailor-made costume, and wears around her neck a silver fox fur*)

NORA (*running in and pushing Peter away from the door*) Oh, can I not turn me back but th' two o' yous are at it like a pair o' fightin'-cocks! Uncle Peter . . . Uncle Peter . . . *Uncle Peter!*

PETER (*vociferously*) Oh, Uncle Peter, Uncle Peter be damned! D'ye think I'm goin' to give a free pass to th' young Covey to turn me whole life into a Holy Manual o' penances an' martyr-doms?

THE COVEY (*angrily rushing into the room*) If you won't exercise some sort o' conthrol over that Uncle Peter o' yours, there'll be a funeral, an' it won't be me that'll be in th' hearse!

NORA (*c back, between Peter and the Covey, to the Covey*) Are yous always goin' to be tearin' down th' little bit of respectability that a body's thryin' to build up? Am I always goin' to be havin' to nurse yous into th' hardy habit o' thryin' to keep up a little bit of appearance?

THE COVEY. Why weren't you here to see th' way he run at me with th' sword?

PETER. What did you call me a lemon-whiskered oul' swine for?

NORA. If th' two o' yous don't thry to make a generous alther-ation in your goin' on, an' keep on thryin' t' inaugurate th' customs o' th' rest o' th' house into this place, yous can flit into other lodgin's where your bowsey battlin' 'ill meet, maybe, with an encore.

(*The* COVEY *comes down, back of the couch to the fire, and sits down in the chair where Peter's shirt had hung; he takes a book from a pocket and begins to read*)

PETER (*to Nora*) Would you like to be called a lemon-whiskered oul' swine?

(NORA *takes the sword from Peter, goes to the table, puts it back in the scabbard, goes to the chest of drawers, back* L, *and leaves it on the chest of drawers*)

NORA (*to Peter*) If you attempt to wag that sword of yours at anybody again, it'll have to be taken off you, an' put in a safe place away from babies that don't know the danger of them things.

(NORA *goes across back, taking off her hat and coat,' which she leaves.* PETER *comes down* C, *takes up the shirt from the floor, and goes back* C *towards the room, back*)

PETER (*at the entrance to the room, back*) Well, I'm not goin' to let anybody call me a lemon-whiskered oul' swine!

(PETER *goes into the room, back.* FLUTHER *moves from the fireplace,* L *of the couch, to the door* L, *which he begins to open and shut, trying the movement*)

FLUTHER (*half to himself, half to Nora*) Openin' an' shuttin' now with a well-mannered motion, like a door of a select bar in a high-class pub.

(NORA *takes up the hat and coat from the table, carries them into the room, back, leaves them there, comes out, goes to the dresser, above the table* R, *and puts a few tea things on the table*)

NORA (*to the Covey, as she lays the table for tea*) An', once for all, Willie, you'll have to thry to deliver yourself from th' desire to practice o' provokin' oul' Pether into a wild forgetfulness of what's proper an' allowable in a respectable home.

THE COVEY. Well, let him mind his own business, then. Yestherday, I caught him hee-hee-in' out of him an' he readin' bits out of Jenersky's *Thesis on th' Origin, Development an' Consolidation of th' Evolutionary Idea of th' Proletariat.*

NORA. Now, let it end at that, for God's sake; Jack'll be in any minute, an' I'm not goin' to have th' quiet of his evenin' tossed about in an everlastin' uproar between you an' Uncle Pether. (*She crosses back to Fluther L, and stands on his R. To Fluther*) Well, did you manage to settle the lock yet, Mr Good?

FLUTHER (*opening and shutting the door*) It's betther than a new one, now, Mrs Clitheroe; it's almost ready to open and shut of its own accord.

NORA (*giving him a coin*) You're a whole man. How many pints will that get you?

FLUTHER (*seriously*) Ne'er a one at all, Mrs Clitheroe, for Fluther's on th' wather waggon now. You could stan' where you're stannin' chantin', 'Have a glass o' malt, Fluther; Fluther, have a glass o' malt,' till th' bells would be ringin' th' ould year out an' th' New Year in, an' you'd have as much chance o' movin' Fluther as a tune on a tin whistle would move a deaf man an' he dead.

(*As NORA is opening and shutting the door, MRS BESSIE BURGESS appears at it. She is a woman of forty, vigorously built. Her face is a dogged one, hardened by toil, and a little coarsened by drink. She looks scornfully and viciously at Nora for a few moments before she speaks*)

BESSIE. Puttin' a new lock on her door . . . afraid her poor neighbours ud break through an' steal . . . (*In a loud tone*) Maybe, now, they're a damn sight more honest than your ladyship . . . checkin' th' children playin' on th' stairs . . . gettin' on th' nerves of your ladyship . . . Complainin' about Bessie Burgess singin' her hymns at night, when she has a few up . . . (*She comes in half-way on the threshold, and screams*) Bessie Burgess 'll sing whenever she damn well likes!

(*NORA tries to shut the door, but BESSIE violently shoves it in, and, gripping Nora by the shoulders, shakes her*)

(*Violently*) You little over-dhressed throllope, you, for one pin, I'd paste th' white face o' you!

NORA (*frightened*) Fluther, Fluther!

FLUTHER (*breaking the hold of Bessie from Nora*) Now, now, Bessie, Bessie, leave poor Mrs Clitheroe alone; she'd do no one any harm, an' minds no one's business but her own.

BESSIE. Why is she always thryin' to speak proud things, an' lookin' like a mighty one in th' congregation o' th' people!

(*The* COVEY *looks up from his book, watches the encounter, but does not leave his seat by the fire.*
NORA *sinks down on the back of the couch.* JACK CLITHEROE *enters by the door,* L. *He is a tall, well-made fellow of twenty-five. His face has none of the strength of Nora's. It is a face in which is the desire for authority, without the power to attain it*)

CLITHEROE (*excitedly*) What's up? what's afther happenin'?
FLUTHER. Nothin', Jack. Nothin'. It's all over now. Come on, Bessie, come on.

CLITHEROE (*coming to the couch and bending over Nora; anxiously*) What's wrong, Nora? Did she say anything to you?

NORA (*agitatedly*) She was bargin' out of her, an' I only told her to go up ower that to her own place; an' before I knew where I was, she flew at me, like a tiger, an' tried to guzzle me.

(CLITHEROE *goes close to Bessie, standing in front of the chest of drawers, and takes hold of her arm to get her away*)

CLITHEROE. Get up to your own place, Mrs Burgess, and don't you be interferin' with my wife, or it'll be th' worse for you . . . Go on, go on!

BESSIE (*as Clitheroe is pushing her out*) Mind who you're pushin', now . . . I attend me place of worship, anyhow . . . Not like some of them that go neither church, chapel or meetin' house . . . If me son was home from the threnches, he'd see me righted.

(FLUTHER *takes* BESSIE *by the arm, and brings her out by the door* L. CLITHEROE *closes the door behind them, returns to Nora, and puts his arm around her. The* COVEY *resumes his reading*)

CLITHEROE (*his arm around her*) There, don't mind that old bitch, Nora, darling; I'll soon put a stop to her interferin'.

NORA. Some day or another, when I'm here be meself, she'll come in an' do somethin' desperate.

CLITHEROE (*kissing her*) Oh, sorra fear of her doin' anythin' desperate. I'll talk to her tomorrow when she's sober. A tast o' me mind that'll shock her into the sensibility of behavin' herself!

(NORA *gets up, crosses to the dresser* R, *and finishes laying the table for tea. She catches sight of the dungarees on the floor and speaks indignantly to the Covey.* CLITHEROE *leaves his hat on the chest of drawers, and sits, waiting for tea, on the couch*)

NORA (*to the Covey*) Willie, is that the place for your dungarees?
THE COVEY (*irritably rising, and taking them from the floor*) Ah, they won't do the floor any harm, will they? (*He carries them up* C, *into the room, back, comes back again, down* C, *and sits by the fire*)

(NORA *crosses from the table to the fire, gets the teapot from the hob, and returns to the table*)

NORA (*to Clitheroe and the Covey*) Tea's ready.

(CLITHEROE *and the* COVEY *go to the table and sit down* L *of same, the* COVEY *nearest the audience.* NORA *sits down on* R *of the table, leaving the chair for Peter below, on the same side*)

(*Calling towards the room, back*) Uncle Peter, Uncle Peter, tea's ready!

(PETER *comes in from the room, back. He is in the full dress of the Irish National Foresters: bright green, gold-braided coat, white breeches, black top boots and frilled, white shirt. He carries a large black slouch hat, from which waves a long white ostrich plume, in his hand. He puts the hat on the chest of drawers beside the sword, comes down* C, *goes round the front end of the table, and sits on the vacant seat facing the Covey on the opposite side of the table. They eat for a few moments in silence, the* COVEY *furtively watching Peter with scorn in his eyes;* PETER *knows this, and is fidgety*)

THE COVEY (*provokingly*) Another cut o' bread, Uncle Peter?

(PETER *maintains a dignified silence*)

CLITHEROE. It's sure to be a great meetin' tonight. We ought to go, Nora.

NORA (*decisively*) I won't go, Jack; you can go if you wish.

(*There is a pause*)

THE COVEY (*with great politeness, to Peter*) D'ye want th' sugar, Uncle Peter?

PETER (*explosively*) Now, are you goin' to start your thryin' an' your twartin' again?

NORA. Now, Uncle Peter, you mustn't be so touchy; Willie has only assed you if you wanted th' sugar.

PETER (*angrily*) He doesn't care a damn whether I want th' sugar or no. He's only thryin' to twart me!

NORA (*angrily, to the Covey*) Can't you let him alone, Willie? If he wants the sugar, let him stretch his hand out an' get it himself!

THE COVEY (*to Peter*) Now, if you want the sugar, you can stretch out your hand and get it yourself!

(*There is a pause*)

CLITHEROE. Tonight is th' first chance that Brennan has got of showing himself off since they made a Captain of him—why, God only knows. It'll be a treat to see him swankin' it at th' head of the Citizen Army carryin' th' flag of the Plough an' th' Stars . . . (*Looking roguishly at Nora*) He was sweet on you, once, Nora?

Nora. He may have been . . . I never liked him. I always thought he was a bit of a thick.

The Covey. They're bringin' nice disgrace on that banner now.

Clitheroe (*to Covey, remonstratively*) How are they bringin' disgrace on it?

The Covey (*snappily*) Because it's a Labour flag, an' was never meant for politics . . . What does th' design of th' field plough, bearin' on it th' stars of th' heavenly plough, mean, if it's not Communism? It's a flag that should only be used when we're buildin' th' barricades to fight for a Workers' Republic!

Peter (*with a puff of derision*) P-phuh.

The Covey (*angrily, to Peter*) What are you phuhin' out o' you for? Your mind is th' mind of a mummy. (*Rising*) I betther go an' get a good place to have a look at Ireland's warriors passin' by.

(*The* Covey *goes into the room* L, *and returns with his cap*)

Nora (*to the Covey*) Oh, Willie, brush your clothes before you go.

The Covey (*carelessly*) Oh, they'll do well enough.

Nora. Go an' brush them; th' brush is in th' drawer there.

(*The* Covey *goes to the drawer, muttering, gets the brush, and starts to brush his clothes*)

The Covey (*reciting at Peter, as he does so*)

> Oh, where's th' slave so lowly,
> Condemn'd to chains unholy,
> Who, could he burst his bonds at first,
> Would pine beneath them slowly?

> We tread th' land that . . . bore us,
> Th' green flag glitters . . . o'er us,
> Th' friends we've tried are by our side,
> An' th' foe we hate . . . before us!

Peter (*leaping to his feet in a whirl of rage*) Now, I'm tellin' you, me young Covey, once for all, that I'll not stick any longer these tittherin' taunts of yours, rovin' around to sing your slights an' slandhers, reddenin' th' mind of a man to th' thinkin' an' sayin' of things that sicken his soul with sin! (*Hysterically; lifting up a cup to fling at the Covey*) Be God, I'll——

Clitheroe (*catching his arm*) Now then, none o' that, none o' that!

Nora (*loudly*) Uncle Pether, Uncle Pether, *Uncle Pether!*

The Covey (*at the door* L, *about to go out*) Isn't that th' malignant oul' varmint! Lookin' like th' illegitimate son of an illegitimate child of a corporal in th' Mexican army!

(*The* Covey *goes out by the door* L)

Peter (*plaintively*) He's afther leavin' me now in such a state of agitation that I won't be able to do meself justice when I'm marchin' to th' meetin'.

(Nora *jumps up from the table, crosses the back end of table to the chest of drawers, back, and takes up Peter's sword*)

Nora. Oh, for God's sake, here, buckle your sword on, an' go to your meetin', so that we'll have at least one hour of peace.

(Peter *gets up from the chair, goes over to* Nora, *and she helps him to put on his sword*)

Clitheroe. For God's sake, hurry him up out o' this, Nora.

Peter. Are yous all goin' to thry to start to twart me now?

Nora (*putting on his plumed hat*) S-s-sh. Now, your hat's on, your house is thatched; off you pop! (*She gently pushes him from her, towards the door* L)

Peter (*going and turning as he reaches the door* L) Now, if that young Covey——

Nora. Go on, go on.

(Peter *goes out by the door* L.

Clitheroe *goes from the table to the couch and sits down on the end nearest the fire, lights a cigarette, and looks thoughtfully into the fire.* Nora *takes things from the table, and puts them on the dresser. She goes into the room, back, and comes back with a lighted shaded lamp, which she puts on the table. She then goes on tidying things on the dresser*)

(*Softly speaking over from the dresser, to Clitheroe*) A penny for them, Jack.

Clitheroe. Me? Oh, I was thinkin' of nothing.

Nora. You were thinkin' of th' . . . meetin' . . . Jack. When we were courtin' an' I wanted you to go, you'd say, 'Oh, to hell with meetin's,' an' that you felt lonely in cheerin' crowds when I was absent. An' we weren't a month married when you began that you couldn't keep away from them.

Clitheroe (*crossly*) Oh, that's enough about th' meetin'. It looks as if you wanted me to go th' way you're talkin'. You were always at me to give up the Citizen Army, an' I gave it up : surely that ought to satisfy you.

Nora (*from dresser*) Aye, you gave it up, because you got the sulks when they didn't make a captain of you. (*She crosses over to Clitheroe, and sits on the couch to his* R. *Softly*) It wasn't for my sake, Jack.

Clitheroe. For your sake or no, you're benefitin' by it, aren't you? I didn't forget this was your birthday, did I? (*He puts his arms around her*) And you liked your new hat; didn't you, didn't you? (*He kisses her rapidly several times*)

NORA (*panting*) Jack, Jack; please, Jack! I thought you were tired of that sort of thing long ago.

CLITHEROE. Well, you're finding out now that I amn't tired of it yet, anyhow. Mrs Clitheroe doesn't want to be kissed, sure she doesn't? (*He kisses her again*) Little, little red-lipped Nora!

NORA (*coquettishly removing his arm from around her*) Oh, yes, your little, little red-lipped Nora's a sweet little girl when th' fit seizes you; but your little, little red-lipped Nora has to clean your boots every mornin', all the same.

CLITHEROE (*with a movement of irritation*) Oh, well, if we're goin' to be snotty!

(*There is a pause*)

NORA. It's lookin' like as if it was you that was goin' to be . . . snotty! Bridlin' up with bittherness, th' minute a body attempts t'open her mouth.

CLITHEROE. Is it any wondher, turnin' a tendher sayin' into a meanin' o' malice an' spite!

NORA. It's hard for a body to be always keepin' her mind bent on makin' thoughts that'll be no longer than th' length of your own satisfaction.

(*There is a pause*)

(*Standing up*) If we're goin' to dhribble th' time away sittin' here like a pair o' cranky mummies, I'd be as well sewin' or doin' something about th' place. (*She looks appealingly at him for a few moments; he doesn't speak. She swiftly sits down beside him, and puts her arm around his neck. Imploringly*) Ah, Jack, don't be so cross!

CLITHEROE (*doggedly*) Cross? I'm not cross; I'm not a bit cross. It was yourself started it.

NORA (*coaxingly*) I didn't mean to say anything out o' th' way. You take a body up too quickly, Jack. (*In an ordinary tone as if nothing of an angry nature had been said*) You didn't offer me me evenin' allowance yet.

(CLITHEROE *silently takes out a cigarette for her and himself and lights both*)

(*Trying to make conversation*) How quiet th' house is now; they must be all out.

CLITHEROE (*rather shortly*) I suppose so.

NORA (*rising from the seat*) I'm longin' to show you me new hat, to see what you think of it. Would you like to see it?

CLITHEROE. Ah, I don't mind.

(NORA *hesitates a moment, then goes up* C *to the chest of drawers, takes the hat out of the box, comes down* C, *stands front of the couch, looks into the mirror on the wall below the fireplace, and fixes the hat on her head. She then turns to face Clitheroe*)

Nora. Well, how does Mr Clitheroe like me new hat?
Clitheroe. It suits you, Nora, it does right enough. (*He stands up, puts his hand beneath her chin, and tilts her head up*)

(Nora *looks at him roguishly. He bends down and kisses her*)

Nora. Here, sit down, an' don't let me hear another cross word out of you for th' rest o' the night.

(*The two sit on the couch again,* Clitheroe *nearest the fire*)

Clitheroe (*his arms round Nora*) Little red-lipped Nora.
Nora (*with a coaxing movement of her body towards him*) Jack!
Clitheroe (*tightening his arms around her*) Well?
Nora. You haven't sung me a song since our honeymoon. Sing me one now, do . . . please, Jack!
Clitheroe. What song? *Since Maggie Went Away?*
Nora. Ah, no, Jack, not that; it's too sad. *When You said You Loved Me.*

(*Clearing his throat,* Clitheroe *thinks for a moment, and then begins to sing.* Nora, *putting an arm around him, nestles her head on his breast and listens delightedly*)

Clitheroe (*singing the verses following to the air of 'When You and I were Young, Maggie'*)

> Th' violets were scenting th' woods, Nora,
>   Displaying their charm to th' bee,
> When I first said I lov'd only you, Nora,
>   An' you said you lov'd only me!

> Th' chestnut blooms gleam'd through th' glade, Nora,
>   A robin sang loud from a tree,
> When I first said I lov'd only you, Nora,
>   An' you said you lov'd only me!

> Th' golden-rob'd daffodils shone, Nora,
>   An' danc'd in th' breeze on th' lea;
> When I first said I lov'd only you, Nora,
>   An' you said you lov'd only me!

> Th' trees, birds an' bees sang a song, Nora,
>   Of happier transports to be,
> When I first said I lov'd only you, Nora,
>   An' you said you lov'd only me!

(Nora *kisses him.*
     A knock is heard at the door, r; *a pause as they listen.* Nora *clings closely to Clitheroe. Another knock, more imperative than the first*)

I wonder who can that be, now?

NORA (*a little nervous*) Take no notice of it, Jack; they'll go away in a minute.

(*Another knock is heard, followed by the voice of* CAPTAIN BRENNAN)

THE VOICE OF CAPT. BRENNAN. Commandant Clitheroe, Commandant Clitheroe, are you there? A message from General Jim Connolly.

CLITHEROE (*taking her arms from round him*) Damn it, it's Captain Brennan.

NORA (*anxiously*) Don't mind him, don't mind, Jack. Don't break our happiness . . . Pretend we're not in . . . Let us forget everything tonight but our two selves!

CLITHEROE (*reassuringly*) Don't be alarmed, darling; I'll just see what he wants, an' send him about his business.

NORA (*tremulously; putting her arms around him*) No, no. Please, Jack; don't open it. Please, for your own little Nora's sake!

CLITHEROE (*taking her arms away and rising to open the door*) Now don't be silly, Nora.

(CLITHEROE *opens the door, and admits a young man in the full uniform of the Irish Citizen Army—green suit; slouch green hat caught up at one side by a small Red Hand badge; Sam Browne belt, with a revolver in the holster. He carries a letter in his hand. When he comes in he smartly salutes Clitheroe. The young man is* CAPTAIN BRENNAN. *He stands in front of the chest of drawers*)

CAPT. BRENNAN (*giving the letter to Clitheroe*) A dispatch from General Connolly.

CLITHEROE (*reading. While he is doing so,* BRENNAN's *eyes are fixed on* NORA, *who droops as she sits on the lounge*) 'Commandant Clitheroe is to take command of the eighth battalion of the I.C.A. which will assemble to proceed to the meeting at nine o'clock. He is to see that all units are provided with full equipment: two days' rations and fifty rounds of ammunition. At two o'clock a.m. the army will leave Liberty Hall for a reconnaissance attack on Dublin Castle.—Com.-Gen. Connolly.' (*In surprise, to Capt. Brennan*) I don't understand this. Why does General Connolly call me Commandant?

CAPT. BRENNAN. Th' Staff appointed you Commandant, and th' General agreed with their selection.

CLITHEROE. When did this happen?

CAPT. BRENNAN. A fortnight ago.

CLITHEROE. How is it word was never sent to me?

CAPT. BRENNAN. Word was sent to you . . . I meself brought it.

CLITHEROE. Who did you give it to, then?

CAPT. BRENNAN (*after a pause*) I think I gave it to Mrs Clitheroe, there.

CLITHEROE. Nora, d'ye hear that?

(NORA *makes no answer*)

(*Standing* C; *there is a note of hardness in his voice*) Nora . . . Captain Brennan says he brought a letter to me from General Connolly, and that he gave it to you . . . Where is it? What did you do with it?

(CAPT. BRENNAN *stands in front of the chest of drawers, and softly whistles 'The Soldiers' Song'*)

N .ᴀ (*running over to him, and pleadingly putting her arms around him*) Jack, please Jack, don't go out tonight an' I'll tell you; I'll explain everything . . . Send him away, an' stay with your own little red-lipp'd Nora.

CLITHEROE (*removing her arms from around him*) None o' this non-sense, now; I want to know what you did with th' letter?

(NORA *goes slowly to the couch and sits down again*)

(*Angrily*) Why didn't you give me th' letter? What did you do with it? . . . (*He goes over and shakes her by the shoulder*) What did you do with th' letter?

NORA (*flaming up and standing on her feet*) I burned it, I burned it! That's what I did with it! Is General Connolly an' th' Citizen Army goin' to be your only care? Is your home goin' to be only a place to rest in? Am I goin' to be only somethin' to provide merry-makin' at night for you? Your vanity 'll be th' ruin of you an' me yet . . . That's what's movin' you: because they've made an officer of you, you'll make a glorious cause of what you're doin', while your little red-lipp'd Nora can go on sittin' here, makin' a companion of th' loneliness of th' night!

CLITHEROE (*fiercely*) You burned it, did you? (*He grips her arm*) Well, me good lady——

NORA. Let go—you're hurtin' me!

CLITHEROE. You deserve to be hurt . . . Any letther that comes to me for th' future, take care that I get it . . . D'ye hear—take care that I get it!

(CLITHEROE *lets* NORA *go, and she sinks down, crying on the couch. He goes to the chest of drawers and takes out a Sam Browne belt, which he puts on, and then puts a revolver in the holster. He puts on his hat, and looks towards Nora*)

(*At the door* L, *about to go out*) You needn't wait up for me; if I'm in at all, it won't be before six in th' morning.

NORA (*bitterly*) I don't care if you never come back!

CLITHEROE (*to Capt. Brennan*) Come along, Ned.

(*They go out; there is a pause.* NORA *pulls the new hat from her head and with a bitter movement flings it to the other end of the room.*

There is a gentle knock at the door L, *which opens, and* MOLLSER *comes into the room. She is about fifteen, but looks to be only about ten, for the ravages of consumption have shrivelled her up. She is pitifully worn, walks feebly, and frequently coughs. She goes over and sits down* L *of Nora)*

MOLLSER *(to Nora)* Mother's gone to th' meetin', an' I was feelin' terrible lonely, so I come down to see if you'd let me sit with you, thinkin' you mightn't be goin' yourself . . . I do be terrible afraid I'll die sometime when I'm be meself . . . I often envy you, Mrs Clitheroe, seein' th' health you have, an' th' lovely place you have here, an'. wondherin' if I'll ever be sthrong enough to be keepin' a home together for a man.

(The faint sound of a band playing is heard in the distance outside in the street)

Oh, this must be some more of the Dublin Fusiliers flyin' off to the front.

(The band, passing in the street outside, is now heard loudly playing as they pass the house. It is the music of a brass band playing a regiment to the boat on the way to the front. The tune that is being played is 'It's a Long Way to Tipperary'; as the band comes to the chorus, the regiment is swinging into the street by Nora's house, and the voices of the soldiers can be heard lustily singing the chorus of the song)

It's a long way to Tipperary, it's a long way to go;
It's a long way to Tipperary, to th' sweetest girl I know!
Good-bye Piccadilly, farewell Leicester Square.
It's a long way to Tipperary, but my heart's right there!

(NORA and MOLLSER remain silently listening. As the chorus ends, and the music is faint in the distance again, BESSIE BURGESS *appears at the door* L, *which Mollser has left open)*

BESSIE *(speaking in towards the room)* There's th' men marchin' out into th' dhread dimness o' danger, while th' lice is crawlin' about feedin' on th' fatness o' th' land! But yous'll not escape from th' arrow that flieth be night, or th' sickness that wasteth be day . . . An' ladyship an' all, as some o' them may be, they'll be scatthered abroad, like th' dust in th' darkness!

(BESSIE goes away; NORA *steals over and quietly shuts the door. She comes back to the lounge and wearily throws herself on it beside Mollser)*

MOLLSER *(after a pause and a cough)* Is there anybody goin', Mrs Clitheroe, with a titther o' sense?

CURTAIN

ACT II

SCENE—*A public-house at the corner of the street in which the meeting is being addressed from Platform No. 1. One end of the house is visible to the audience. Part of the counter at the back,* L, *extending out towards* L, *occupies one-third of the width of the scene from* R *to* L. *On the counter are glasses, beer-pulls, and a carafe filled with water. Behind the counter, on the back wall, are shelves containing bottles of wine, whiskey and beer. At back* C *is a wide, high, plate-glass window. Under the window is a seat to hold three or four persons seated.* L *are the wide swing-doors. At the wall,* R, *is a seat to hold two persons. There are a few gaudy coloured show-cards on the walls.*
(See the Ground Plan)

A band is heard outside playing 'The Soldiers' Song', before the CURTAIN *rises, and for a few moments afterwards, accompanied by the sounds of marching men.*
The BARMAN *is seen wiping the part of the counter which is in view.* ROSIE REDMOND *is standing at the counter toying with what remains of a half of whiskey in a wine-glass. She is a sturdy, well-shaped girl of twenty; pretty and pert in manner. She is wearing a cream blouse, with an obviously suggestive glad neck; a grey tweed dress, brown stockings and shoes. The blouse and most of the dress are hidden by a black shawl. She has no hat, and in her hair is jauntily set a cheap, glittering, jewelled ornament. It is an hour later.*

BARMAN *(wiping the counter)* Nothin' much doin' in your line tonight, Rosie?

ROSIE. Curse o' God on th' haporth, hardly, Tom. There isn't much notice taken of a pretty petticoat of a night like this . . . They're all in a holy mood. Th' solemn-lookin' dials on th' whole o' them an' they marchin' to th' meetin'. You'd think they were th' glorious company of th' saints, an' th' noble army of martyrs thrampin' through th' sthreets of Paradise. They're all thinkin' of higher things than a girl's garthers . . . It's a tremendous meetin'; four platforms they have—there's one o' them just outside opposite th' window.

BARMAN. Oh, ay; sure when th' speaker comes *(motioning with his hand)* to th' near end, here, you can see him plain, an' hear nearly everythin' he's spoutin' out of him.

ROSIE. It's no joke thryin' to make up fifty-five shillin's a week for your keep an' laundhry, an' then taxin' you a quid for your own room if you bring home a friend for th' night . . . If I could only put by a couple of quid for a swankier outfit, everythin' in th' garden ud look lovely——

(*In the window, back, appears the figure of a tall man, who, standing on a platform, is addressing a crowd outside. The figure is almost like a silhouette. The* BARMAN *comes to the* L *end of the counter to listen, and* ROSIE *moves* C *to see and listen too*)

BARMAN (*to Rosie*) Whisht, till we hear what he's sayin'.

THE VOICE OF THE MAN. It is a glorious thing to see arms in the hands of Irishmen. We must accustom ourselves to the thought of arms, we must accustom ourselves to the sight of arms, we must accustom ourselves to the use of arms . . . Bloodshed is a cleansing and sanctifying thing, and the nation that regards it as the final horror has lost its manhood . . . There are many things more horrible than bloodshed, and slavery is one of them !

(*The figure, moving towards* L, *passes the window, and is lost to sight and hearing. The* BARMAN *goes back to wiping of the counter.* ROSIE *remains looking out of the window*)

ROSIE. It's th' sacred thruth, mind you, what that man's afther sayin'.

BARMAN. If I was only a little younger, I'd be plungin' mad into th' middle of it !

ROSIE (*who is still looking out of the window*) Oh, here's th' two gems runnin' over again for their oil !

(*The doors* L *swing open, and* FLUTHER *and* PETER *enter tumultuously. They are hot and hasty with the things they have seen and heard. They hurry across to the counter,* PETER *leading the way.* ROSIE, *after looking at them listlessly for a moment, retires to the seat under the window, sits down, takes a cigarette from her pocket, lights it and smokes*)

PETER (*splutteringly to the Barman*) Two halves . . . (*To Fluther*) A meetin' like this always makes me feel as if I could dhrink Loch Erinn dhry !

FLUTHER. You couldn't feel anyway else at a time like this when th' spirit of a man is pulsin' to be out fightin' for th' thruth with his feet thremblin' on th' way, maybe to th' gallows, an' his ears tinglin' with th' faint, far-away sound of burstin' rifle-shots that'll maybe whip th' last little shock o' life out of him that's left lingerin' in his body !

PETER. I felt a burnin' lump in me throat when I heard th' band playin' *The Soldiers' Song*, rememberin' last hearin' it marchin' in military formation, with th' people starin' on both sides at us, carryin' with us th' pride an' resolution o' Dublin to th' grave of Wolfe Tone.

FLUTHER. Get th' Dublin men goin' an' they'll go on full force for anything that's thryin' to bar them away from what they're wantin', where th' slim thinkin' counthry boyo ud limp away from th' first faintest touch of compromization !

PETER (*hurriedly to the Barman*) Two more, Tom! . . . (*To Fluther*) Th' memory of all th' things that was done, an' all th' things that was suffered be th' people, was boomin' in me brain . . . Every nerve in me body was quiverin' to do somethin' desperate!

FLUTHER. Jammed as I was in th' crowd, I listened to th' speeches pattherin' on th' people's head, like rain fallin' on th' corn; every derogatory thought went out o' me mind, an' I said to meself, 'You can die now, Fluther, for you've seen th' shadow-dhreams of th' past leppin' to life in th' bodies of livin' men that show, if we were without a titther o' courage for centuries, we're vice versa now!' Looka here. (*He stretches out his arm under Peter's face and rolls up his sleeve*) The blood was *boilin'* in me veins!

(*The silhouette of the tall figure again moves into the frame of the window, speaking to the people*)

PETER (*unaware, in his enthusiasm, of the speaker's appearance; to Fluther*) I was burnin' to dhraw me sword, an' wave it over me——

FLUTHER (*overwhelming Peter*) Will you stop your blatherin' for a minute, man, an' let us hear what he's sayin'!

(*The* BARMAN *comes to the* L *end of the counter to look at the figure in the window:* ROSIE *rises from the seat, stands and looks.* FLUTHER *and* PETER *move towards* C *to see and listen*)

THE VOICE OF THE MAN. Comrade soldiers of the Irish Volunteers and of the Citizen Army, we rejoice in this terrible war. The old heart of the earth needed to be warmed with the red wine of the battlefields . . . Such august homage was never offered to God as this: the homage of millions of lives given gladly for love of country. And we must be ready to pour out the same red wine in the same glorious sacrifice, for without shedding of blood there is no redemption!

(*The figure moves out of sight and hearing.*
FLUTHER *runs back to the counter and gulps down the drink remaining in his glass;* PETER *does the same, less rapidly; the* BARMAN *leaves the end of the counter;* ROSIE *sits on the seat again*)

FLUTHER (*finishing his drink; to Peter*) Come on, man; this is too good to be missed!

(FLUTHER *rushes across the stage and out by the doors* L. PETER *wipes his mouth and hurries after Fluther. The doors swing open, and the* COVEY *enters. He collides with* PETER C. PETER *stiffens his body, like a cock, and, with a look of hatred on his face, marches stiffly out by the doors* L. *The* COVEY *looks scornfully after Peter, and then crosses to the counter.* ROSIE *sees possibilities in the Covey, gets up and comes to the counter, a little to the* L *of the Covey*)

THE COVEY (*to the Barman*) Give us a glass o' malt, for God's sake, till I stimulate meself from the shock of seeing the sight that's afther goin' out.

ROSIE (*slyly, to the Barman*) Another one for me, Tommy; the young gentleman's ordherin' it in the corner of his eye.

(*The* BARMAN *gets a drink for the Covey, leaves it on the counter ;* ROSIE *whips it up. The* BARMAN *catches Rosie's arm, and takes the glass from her, putting it down beside the Covey*)

BARMAN (*taking the glass from Rosie*) Eh, houl' on there, houl' on there Rosie.

ROSIE (*angrily, to the Barman*) What are you houldin' on out o' you for? Didn't you hear th' young gentleman say that he couldn't refuse anything to a nice little bird? (*To the Covey*) Isn't that right, Jiggs?

(*The* COVEY *says nothing*)

Didn't I know, Tommy, it would be all right? It takes Rosie to size a young man up, an' tell th' thoughts that are thremblin' in his mind. Isn't that right, Jiggs?

(*The* COVEY *stirs uneasily, moves a little farther away, and pulls his cap over his eyes*)

(*Moving after him*) Great meetin' that's gettin' held outside. Well, it's up to us all, anyway, to fight for our freedom.

THE COVEY (*to the Barman*) Two more, please. (*To Rosie*) Freedom! What's th' use o' freedom, if it's not economic freedom?

ROSIE (*emphasizing with extended arm and moving finger*) I used them very words just before you come in. 'A lot o' thricksters,' says I, 'that wouldn't know what freedom was if they got it from their mother' . . . (*To the Barman*) Didn't I, Tommy?

BARMAN. I disremember.

ROSIE (*to the Barman*) No, you don't disremember. Remember you said, yourself, it was all 'only a flash in th' pan'. Well, 'flash in th' pan, or no flash in th' pan,' says I, 'they're not goin' to get Rosie Redmond,' says I, 'to fight for freedom that wouldn't be worth winnin' in a raffle!'

THE COVEY (*contemptuously*) There's only one freedom for th' workin' man: conthrol o' th' means o' production, rates of exchange an' th' means of disthribution. (*Tapping Rosie on the shoulder*) Look here, comrade, I'll leave here tomorrow night for you a copy of Jenersky's *Thesis on the Origin, Development an' Consolidation of the Evolutionary Idea of th' Proletariat.*

ROSIE (*throwing off her shawl on to the counter, and showing an exemplified glad neck, which reveals a good deal of a white bosom*) If y'ass Rosie, it's heartbreakin' to see a young fella thinkin' of anything, or admirin' anything, but silk thransparent stockin's showin' off the shape of a little lassie's legs!

(*The* Covey *is frightened, and moves away from* Rosie *along the counter, towards* r. Rosie *follows, gliding after him in a seductive way*)

(*Following him*) Out in th' park in th' shade of a warm summery evenin', with your little darlin' bridie to be, kissin' an' cuddlin' (*she tries to put her arm around his neck*), kissin' an' cuddlin', ay?

The Covey (*frightened*) Ay, what are you doin'? None o' that, now; none o' that. I've something else to do besides shinanickin' afther Judies!

(*The* Covey *turns to* l *and moves slowly to* l, *away from* Rosie; *she turns with him, keeping him facing her, holding his arm. They move this way to* c)

Rosie. Oh, little duckey, oh, shy little duckey! Never held a mot's hand, an' wouldn't know how to tittle a little Judy! (*She clips him under the chin*) Tittle him undher th' chin, tittle him undher th' chin!

The Covey (*breaking away and running out by the doors* l) Aye, go on, now; I don't want to have any meddlin' with a lassie like you!

Rosie (*enraged; returning to the seat at the window*) Jasus, it's in a monasthery some of us ought to be, spendin' our holidays kneelin' on our adorers, tellin' our beads an' knockin' hell out of our buzzums!

(*The voice of the* Covey *is heard outside the doors* l *calling in a scale of notes,* 'Cuckoo-ooooo.' *Then the swing-doors open, and* Peter *and* Fluther, *followed by* Mrs Gogan, *come in.* Mrs Gogan *carries a baby in her arms*)

Peter (*in plaintive anger, looking towards the door* l) It's terrible that young Covey can't let me pass without proddin' at me! Did you hear him murmurin' 'cuckoo' when he were passin'?

Fluther (*irritably; to Peter*) I wouldn't be everlastin' cockin' me ear to hear every little whisper that was floatin' around about me! It's my rule never to lose me temper till it would be dethrimental to keep it. There's nothin' derogatory in th' use o' th' word 'cuckoo', is there?

(Mrs Gogan, *followed by* Peter, *goes up to the seat under the window and sits down, Peter to the* r *of Mrs Gogan.* Rosie, *after a look at those who've come in, goes out by the doors* l)

Peter (*tearfully*) It's not the word, it's the way he says it! He never says it straight out, but murmurs it with curious quiverin' ripples, like variations on a flute.

Fluther (*standing in front of the seat*) A' what odds if he gave it

with variations on a thrombone? (*To Mrs Gogan*) What's yours
goin' to be, maam?

MRS GOGAN. Ah, half a malt, Fluther.

(FLUTHER *goes from the seat over to the counter*)

FLUTHER (*to the Barman*) Three halves, Tommy.

(*The* BARMAN *gets the drinks, and leaves them on the counter.*
FLUTHER *pays the Barman; takes the drinks to the seat under the
the window; gives one to Mrs Gogan, one to Peter, and keeps the third
for himself. He then sits on the seat to the* L *of Mrs Gogan*)

MRS GOGAN (*drinking, and looking admiringly at Peter's costume*)
The Foresthers' is a gorgeous dhress! I don't think I've seen
nicer, mind you, in a pantomime . . . Th' loveliest part of th'
dhress, I think, is th' osthrichess plume . . . When yous are goin'
along, an' I see them wavin' an' noddin' an' waggin', I seem
to be lookin' at each of yous hangin' at th' end of a rope, your
eyes bulgin' an' your legs twistin' an' jerkin', gaspin' an' gaspin'
for breath while yous are thryin' to die for Ireland!

FLUTHER (*scornfully*) If any o' them is ever hangin' at the end
of a rope, it won't be for Ireland!

PETER. Are you goin' to start th' young Covey's game o'
proddin' an' twartin' a man? There's not many that's talkin' can
say that for twenty-five years he never missed a pilgrimage to
Bodenstown!

FLUTHER (*looking angrily at Peter*) You're always blowin' about
goin' to Bodenstown. D'ye think no one but yourself ever went
to *Bodenstown?* (*He emphasizes the word 'Bodenstown'*)

PETER (*plaintively*) I'm not blowin' about it; but there's not
a year that I go there but I pluck a leaf off Tone's grave, an' this
very day me prayer-book is nearly full of them.

FLUTHER (*scornfully*) Then Fluther has a vice-versa opinion of
them that put ivy leaves into their prayer-books, scabbin' it on th'
clergy, an' thryin' to out-do th' haloes o' th' saints be lookin' as
if he was wearin' around his head a glittherin' aroree boree allis!
(*Fiercely*) Sure, I don't care a damn if you slep' in *Bodenstown!*
You can take your breakfast, dinner an' tea on th' grave, in
Bodenstown, if you like, for Fluther!

MRS GOGAN. Oh, don't start a fight, boys, for God's sake; I
was only sayin' what a nice costume it is—nicer than th' kilts, for,
God forgive me, I always think th' kilts is hardly decent.

FLUTHER (*laughing scornfully*) Ah, sure, when you'd look at
him, you'd wondher whether th' man was makin' fun o' th'
costume, or th' costume was makin' fun o' th' man!

BARMAN (*over to them*) Now, then, thry to speak asy, will yous?
We don't want no shoutin' here.

(*The swing-doors open and the* COVEY, *followed by* BESSIE
BURGESS, *comes in. They go over and stand at the counter. Passing,*

BESSIE *gives a scornful look at those seated near the window.* BESSIE *and the* COVEY *talk together, but frequently eye the group at the window)*

COVEY (*to the Barman*) Two glasses o' malt.

(*The* BARMAN *gets the drinks and leaves them on the counter. The* COVEY *puts one beside Bessie and keeps the other. He pays the Barman*)

PETER (*plaintively*) There he is now—I knew he wouldn't be long till he folleyed me in.

BESSIE (*speaking to the Covey, but really at the other party*) I can't for th' life o' me undherstand how they can call themselves Catholics, when they won't lift a finger to help poor little Catholic Belgium.

MRS GOGAN (*raising her voice*) What about poor little Catholic Ireland?

BESSIE (*over to Mrs Gogan*) You mind your own business, maam, an' stupify your foolishness be gettin' dhrunk.

PETER (*anxiously; to Mrs Gogan*) Take no notice of her; pay no attention to her. She's just tormentin' herself towards havin' a row with somebody.

BESSIE (*in quiet anger*) There's a storm of anger tossin' in me heart, thinkin' of all th' poor Tommies, an' with them me own son, dhrenched in water an' soaked in blood, gropin' their way to a shattherin' death, in a shower o' shells! Young men with th' sunny lust o' life beamin' in them, layin' down their white bodies, shredded into torn an' bloody pieces, on th' althar that God Himself has built for th' sacrifice of heroes!

MRS GOGAN (*indignantly*) Isn't it a nice thing to have to be listenin' to a lassie an' hangin' our heads in a dead silence, knowin' that some persons think more of a ball of malt than they do of th' blessed saints.

FLUTHER (*deprecatingly*) Whisht; she's always dangerous an' derogatory when she's well oiled. Th' safest way to hindher her from havin' any enjoyment out of her spite, is to dip our thoughts into the fact of her bein' a female person that has moved out of th' sight of ordinary sensible people.

BESSIE (*over to Mrs Gogan; viciously*) To look at some o' th' women that's knockin' about, now, is a thing to make a body sigh . . . A woman on her own, dhrinkin' with a bevy o' men is hardly an example to her sex . . . A woman dhrinkin' with a woman is one thing, an' a woman dhrinkin' with herself is still a woman— flappers may be put in another category altogether— but a middle-aged married woman makin' herself th' centre of a circle of men is as a woman that is loud an' stubborn, whose feet abideth not in her own house.

THE COVEY (*to Bessie; with a scornful look at Peter*) When I think of all th' problems in front o' th' workers, it makes me sick to be lookin' at oul' codgers goin' about dhressed up like green-accoutered figures gone asthray out of a toyshop!

PETER (angrily) Gracious God, give me patience to be listenin' to that blasted young Covey proddin' at me from over at th' other end of th' shop!

MRS GOGAN (dipping her finger in the whiskey, and moistening with it the lips of her baby) Cissie Gogan's a woman livin' for nigh on twenty-five years in her own room, an' beyond biddin' th' time o' day to her neighbours, never yet as much as nodded her head in th' direction of other people's business, while she knows some (with a look at Bessie) as are never content unless they're standin' senthry over other people's doin's!

(Again the figure appears, like a silhouette, in the window, back, and all hear the voice of the speaker declaiming passionately to the gathering outside. FLUTHER, PETER and MRS GOGAN stand up, turn, and look towards the window. The BARMAN comes to the end of the counter; BESSIE and the COVEY stop talking, and look towards the window)

THE VOICE OF THE SPEAKER. The last sixteen months have been the most glorious in the history of Europe. Heroism has come back to the earth. War is a terrible thing, but war is not an evil thing. People in Ireland dread war because they do not know it. Ireland has not known the exhilaration of war for over a hundred years. When war comes to Ireland she must welcome it as she would welcome the Angel of God!

(The figure passes out of sight and hearing, L)

THE COVEY (towards all present) Dope, dope. There's only one war worth havin': th' war for th' economic emancipation of th' proletariat.

BESSIE (referring to Mrs Gogan) They may crow away out o' them; but it ud be fitther for some o' them to mend their ways, an' cease from havin' scouts out watchin' for th' comin' of th' Saint Vincent de Paul man, for fear they'd be nailed lowerin' a pint of beer, mockin' th' man with an angel face, shinin' with th' glamour of deceit an' lies!

MRS GOGAN (over to Bessie) An' a certain lassie standin' stiff behind her own door with her ears cocked listenin' to what's being said, stuffed till she's sthrained with envy of a neighbour thryin' for a few little things that may be got be hard sthrivin' to keep up to th' letther an' th' law, an' th' practices of th' Church!

PETER (to Mrs Gogan) If I was you, Mrs Gogan, I'd parry her jabbin' remarks be a powerful silence that'll keep her tantalizin' words from penethratin' into your feelin's. It's always betther to leave these people to th' vengeance o' God!

BESSIE (at the counter) Bessie Burgess doesn't put up to know much, never havin' a swaggerin' mind, thanks be to God, but goin' on packin' up knowledge accordin' to her conscience: precept upon precept, line upon line; here a little, an' there a little.

(BESSIE, *with a vigorous swing of her shawl, turns, and with a quick movement goes* C, *facing Mrs Gogan*)

(*Furiously*) But, thanks be to Christ, she knows when she was got, where she was got, an' how she was got; while there's some she knows, decoratin' their finger with a well-polished weddin' ring, would be hard put to it if they were assed to show their weddin' lines!

(MRS GOGAN *springs up from the seat and bounces to* C, *facing Bessie Burgess.* MRS GOGAN *is wild with anger*)

MRS GOGAN (*with hysterical rage*) Y' oul' rip of a blasted liar, me weddin' ring's been well earned be twenty years be th' side o' me husband, now takin' his rest in heaven, married to me be Father Dempsey, in th' Chapel o' Saint Jude's, in th' Christmas Week of eighteen hundhred an' ninety-five; an' any kid, livin' or dead, that Jinnie Gogan's had since, was got between th' bordhers of th' Ten Commandments! . . .

BESSIE (*bringing the palms of her hands together in sharp claps to emphasize her remarks*) Liar to you, too, maam, y' oul' hardened thresspasser on other people's good nature, wizenin' up your soul in th' arts o' dodgeries, till every dhrop of respectability in a female is dhried up in her, lookin' at your ready-made manœuverin' with th' menkind!

BARMAN (*anxiously leaning over the counter*) Here, there; here, there; speak asy there. No rowin' here, no rowin' here, now.

(FLUTHER *comes from the seat, gets in front of Mrs Gogan, and tries to pacify her;* PETER *leaves the seat, and tries to do the same with Bessie, holding her back from Mrs Gogan. The positions are:* BARMAN *behind the counter, leaning forward;* BESSIE R; *next* PETER; *next* FLUTHER; *next* MRS GOGAN, *with baby in her arms. The* COVEY *remains leaning on the counter, looking on*)

FLUTHER (*trying to calm Mrs Gogan*) Now, Jinnie, Jinnie, it's a derogatory thing to be smirchin' a night like this with a row; it's rompin' with th' feelin's of hope we ought to be, instead o' bein' vice versa!

PETER (*trying to quiet Bessie*) I'm terrible dawny, Mrs Burgess, an' a fight leaves me weak for a long time afterwards . . . Please, Mrs Burgess, before there's damage done, thry to have a little respect for yourself.

BESSIE (*with a push of her hand that sends* PETER *tottering to the end of the counter*) G'way, you little sermonizing, little yella-faced, little consequential, little pudgy, little bum, you!

MRS GOGAN (*screaming and struggling*) Fluther, leggo! I'm not goin' to keep an unresistin' silence, an' her scatherin' her festherin' words in me face, stirrin' up every dhrop of decency in a respectable female, with her restless rally o' lies that would make a saint say his prayer backwards!

BESSIE (*shouting*) Ah, everybody knows well that th' best charity that can be shown to you is to hide th' thruth as much as our thrue worship of God Almighty will allow us!

MRS GOGAN (*frantically*) Here, houl' th' kid, one o' yous; houl' th' kid for a minute! There's nothin' for it but to show this lassie a lesson or two . . . (*To Peter*) Here, houl' th' kid, you.

(MRS GOGAN *suddenly rushes over to* PETER, *standing, trembling with fear, between the end of the counter and the seat under the window. Bewildered, and before he's aware of it,* MRS GOGAN *has put the baby in his arms.* MRS GOGAN *rushes back* C *and puts herself in a fighting attitude in front of Bessie*)

(*To Bessie, standing before her in a fighting attitude*) Come on, now, me loyal lassie, dyin' with grief for little Catholic Belgium! When Jinnie Gogan's done with you, you'll have a little leisure lyin' down to think an' pray for your king an' counthry!

BARMAN (*coming from behind the counter, getting between the women, and proceeding to push Bessie towards the door*) Here, now, since yous can't have a little friendly argument quietly, yous'll get out o' this place in quick time. Go on, an' settle your differences somewhere else—I don't want to have another endorsement on me licence.

(*The* BARMAN *pushes Bessie towards the doors* L, MRS GOGAN *following*)

PETER (*anxiously calling to Mrs Gogan*) Here, take your kid back ower this. How nicely I was picked now for it to be plumped into my arms!

THE COVEY (*meaningly*) She knew who she was givin' it to, maybe.

(PETER *goes over near to the Covey at the counter to retort indignantly, as the* BARMAN *pushes Bessie out of the doors* L *and gets hold of Mrs Gogan to put her out too*)

PETER (*hotly to the Covey*) Now, I'm givin' you fair warnin', me young Covey, to quit firin' your jibes an' jeers at me . . . For one o' these days, I'll run out in front o' God Almighty an' take your sacred life!

BARMAN (*pushing Mrs Gogan out after Bessie*) Go on, now; out you go.

PETER (*leaving the baby down on the floor* C) Ay, be Jasus, wait there, till I give her back her youngster! (*He runs to the door* L, *opens it, and calls out after Mrs Gogan. Calling at the door* L) Eh, there, eh! What about the kid? (*He runs back in,* C, *and looks at Fluther and the*

Covey) There, she's afther goin' without her kid—what are we goin' to do with it now?
THE COVEY (*jeering*) What are *you* goin' to do with it? Bring it outside an' show everybody what you're afther findin'.
PETER (*in a panic; to Fluther*) Pick it up, you, Fluther, an' run afther her with it, will you?
FLUTHER (*with a long look at Peter*) What d'ye take Fluther for? You must think Fluther's a right gom. D'ye think Fluther's like yourself, destitute of a titther of undherstandin'?
BARMAN (*imperatively to Peter*) Take it up, man, an' run out afther her with it, before she's gone too far. You're not goin' to leave th' bloody thing there, are you?
PETER (*plaintively, as he lifts up the baby*) Well, God Almighty, give me patience with all th' scorners, tormentors, an' twarters that are always an' ever thryin' to goad me into prayin' for their blindin' an' blastin' an' burnin' in th' world to come!

(PETER, *with the baby, goes out of the door* L. FLUTHER *comes from the front of the window to the counter and stands there, beside the* Covey)

FLUTHER (*with an air of relief*) God, it's a relief to get rid o' that crowd. Women is terrible when they start to fight. There's no holdin' them back. (*To the Covey*) Are you goin' to have anything?
THE COVEY. Ah, I don't mind if I have another half.
FLUTHER (*to the Barman*) Two more, Tommy, me son.

(*The* BARMAN *gets the drinks,* FLUTHER *pays*)

(*To the Covey*) You know there's no conthrollin' a woman when she loses her head.

(ROSIE *appears at the doors* L. *She looks over at the counter, sees the two men, then crosses over to the* L *end of the counter, where she stands, with a suggestive look towards Fluther*)

ROSIE (*to the Barman*) Divil a use o' havin' a thrim little leg on a night like this; thin₃s was never worse . . . Give us a half till tomorrow, Tom, duckey.
BARMAN (*coldly*) No more tonight, Rosie; you owe me for three already.
ROSIE (*combatively*) You'll be paid, won't you?
BARMAN. I hope so.
ROSIE. You hope so! Is that th' way with you, now?
FLUTHER (*with a long glance at Rosie; to the Barman*) Give her one—it'll be all right.

(*The* BARMAN *gets a drink, and puts it on the counter before Rosie;* FLUTHER *pays for it*)

ROSIE (*clapping Fluther on the back*) Oul' sport!
FLUTHER (*to the Covey*) Th' meetin' should be soon over, now.

THE COVEY (*in a superior way*) Th' sooner th' betther. It's all a lot o' blasted nonsense, comrade.

FLUTHER. Oh, I wouldn't say it was all nonsense. Afther all, Fluther can remember th' time, an' him only a dawny chiselur, bein' taught at his mother's knee to be faithful to th' Shan Vok Vok!

THE COVEY. That's all dope, comrade; th' sort o' thing that workers are fed on be th' Boorzwawzee.

FLUTHER (*a little sharply*) What's all dope? Though I'm sayin' it that shouldn't—(*catching his cheek with his hand, and pulling down the flesh from the eye*) d'ye see that mark there, undher me eye? . . . A sabre slice from a dragoon in O'Connell Street! (*Thrusting his head forward towards Rosie*) Feel that dint in th' middle o' me nut!

ROSIE (*rubbing Fluther's head, and winking at the Covey*) My God, there's a holla!

FLUTHER (*putting on his hat with quiet pride*) A skelp from a bobby's baton at a Labour meetin' in th' Phœnix Park!

THE COVEY (*sarcastically*) He must ha' hitten you in mistake. I don't know what you ever done for th' Labour movement.

FLUTHER (*loudly*) D'ye not? Maybe, then, I done as much, an' know as much about th' Labour movement as th' chancers that are blowin' about it!

BARMAN (*over the counter*) Speak easy, Fluther, thry to speak easy.

THE COVEY (*quietly*) There's no necessity to get excited about it, comrade.

FLUTHER (*more loudly*) Excited? Who's gettin' excited? There's no one gettin' excited! It would take something more than a thing like you to flutther a feather o' Fluther. Blatherin', an', when all is said, you know as much as th' rest in th' wind up!

THE COVEY (*emphatically*) Well, let us put it to th' test, then, an' see what you know about th' Labour movement: what's the mechanism of exchange?

FLUTHER (*roaring, because he feels he is beaten*) How th' hell do I know what it is? There's nothin' about that in th' rules of our Thrades Union!

BARMAN (*protestingly*) For God's sake, thry to speak easy, Fluther.

THE COVEY. What does Karl Marx say about th' Relation of Value to th' Cost o' Production?

FLUTHER (*angrily*) What th' hell do I care what he says? I'm Irishman enough not to lose me head be follyin' foreigners!

BARMAN. Speak easy, Fluther.

THE COVEY (*contemptuously*) It's only waste o' time talkin' to you, comrade.

FLUTHER. Don't be comradin' me, mate. I'd be on me last legs if I wanted you for a comrade.

ROSIE (*to the Covey, taking Fluther's part*) It seems a highly ridiculous thing to hear a thing that's only an inch or two away from a kid, swingin' heavy words about he doesn't know th' meanin' of, an' uppishly thryin' to down a man like Misther Fluther here, that's well flavoured in th' knowledge of th' world he's livin' in.

THE COVEY (*bending over the counter; savagely to Rosie*) Nobody's askin' you to be buttin' in with your prate . . . I have you well taped, me lassie . . . Just you keep your opinions for your own place . . . It'll be a long time before th' Covey takes any insthructions or reprimandin' from a prostitute!

(ROSIE, *wild with humiliation, bounds from the end of the counter to* C *and with eyes blazing, faces towards the Covey*)

ROSIE. You louse, you louse, you! . . . You're no man . . . You're no man . . . I'm a woman, anyhow, an' if I'm a prostitute aself, I have me feelin's . . . Thryin' to put his arm around me a minute ago, an' giving me th' glad eye, th' little wrigglin' lump o' desolation turns on me now, because he saw there was nothin' doin' . . . You louse, you! If I was a man, or you were a woman, I'd bate th' puss o' you!

BARMAN. Ay, Rosie, ay! You'll have to shut your mouth altogether, if you can't learn to speak easy!

(FLUTHER, *with a dignified walk, goes over to Rosie* C, *and puts a hand on her shoulder*)

FLUTHER (*to Rosie*) Houl' on there, Rosie; houl' on, there. There's no necessity to flutther yourself when you're with Fluther . . . Any lady that's in th' company of Fluther is goin' to get a fair hunt . . . This is outside your province . . . I'm not goin' to let you demean yourself be talkin' to a tittherin' chancer . . . Leave this to Fluther—this is a man's job . . . (*He turns from Rosie, comes back, crosses the Covey, then turns and faces him. To the Covey*) Now, if you've anything to say, say it to Fluther; an' let me tell you, you're not goin' to be pass-remarkable to any lady in my company.

THE COVEY. Sure I don't care if you were runnin' all night afther your Mary o' th' Curlin' Hair, but, when you start tellin' luscious lies about what you done for th' Labour movement, it's nearly time to show y'up!

FLUTHER (*fiercely*) Is it you show Fluther up? G'way, man, I'd beat two o' you before me breakfast!

THE COVEY (*contemptuously*) Tell us where you bury your dead, will you?

FLUTHER (*with his face stuck into the face of the Covey*) Sing a little less on th' high note, or, when I'm done with you, you'll put a Christianable consthruction on things, I'm tellin' you!

THE COVEY. You're a big fella, you are.

FLUTHER (*tapping the Covey threateningly on the shoulder*) Now, you're temptin' Providence when you're temptin' Fluther!

THE COVEY (*losing his temper, knocking Fluther's hands away, and bawling*) Easy with them hands, there, easy with them hands! You're startin' to take a little risk when you commence to paw the Covey!

(FLUTHER *suddenly springs into the* C *of the shop, flings his hat into the corner, whips off his coat, and begins to paw the air like a pugilist*)

FLUTHER (*roaring*) Come on, come on, you lowser; put your mits up now, if there's a man's blood in you! Be God, in a few minutes you'll see some snots flyin' around, I'm tellin' you . . . When Fluther's done with you, you'll have a vice-versa opinion of him! Come on, now, come on!

(*The* COVEY *squares up to Fluther*)

BARMAN (*running from behind the counter and catching hold of the Covey*) Here, out you go, me little bowsey. Because you got a couple o' halves you think you can act as you like. (*He pushes the Covey to the doors* L) Fluther's a friend o' mine, an' I'll not have him insulted.

THE COVEY (*struggling with the Barman*) Ay, leggo, leggo there; fair hunt, give a man a fair hunt! One minute with him is all I ask; one minute alone with him, while you're runnin' for th' priest an' th' doctor!

FLUTHER (*to the Barman*) Let him go, let him go, Tom: let him open th' door to sudden death if he wants to!

BARMAN (*grappling with the Covey*) Go on, out you go an' do th' bowsey somewhere else.

(*The* BARMAN *pushes the* COVEY *out by the doors* L, *and goes back behind the counter.* FLUTHER *assumes a proud air of victory.* ROSIE *gets his coat, and helps him to put it on; she then gets his hat and puts it on his head*)

ROSIE (*helping Fluther with his coat*) Be God, you put th' fear o' God in his heart that time! I thought you'd have to be dug out of him . . . Th' way you lepped out without any of your fancy side-steppin'! 'Men like Fluther,' says I to meself, 'is gettin' scarce nowadays.'

FLUTHER (*with proud complacency,* C) I wasn't goin' to let meself be malignified by a chancer . . . He got a little bit too derogatory for Fluther . . . Be God, to think of a cur like that comin' to talk to a man like me!

ROSIE (*fixing on his hat*) Did j'ever!

FLUTHER. He's lucky he got off safe. I hit a man last week, Rosie, an' he's fallin' yet!

Rosie. Sure, you'd ha' broken him in two if you'd ha' hitten him one clatther!

Fluther (*amorously, putting his arm around Rosie*) Come on into th' snug, me little darlin', an' we'll have a few dhrinks before I see you home.

Rosie. Oh, Fluther, I'm afraid you're a terrible man for th' women.

(Fluther *leads* Rosie *to the seat with the round table in front,* r. *She sits down on the seat. He goes to the counter*)

Fluther (*to the Barman*) Two, full ones, Tommy.

(*The* Barman *gets the drinks.* Fluther *brings them over to the seat* r, *leaves them on the table, and sits down beside Rosie.*

The swing-doors l *open and* Captain Brennan, Commandant Clitheroe, *and* Lieutenant Langon *enter, and cross quickly to the counter.* Capt. Brennan *carries the banner of The Plough and the Stars, and* Lieut. Langon *a green, white and orange Tricolour. They are in a state of emotional excitement. Their faces are flushed and their eyes sparkle; they speak rapidly, as if unaware of the meaning of what they say. They have been mesmerized by the fervency of the speeches*)

Clitheroe (*almost pantingly to the Barman*) Three glasses o' port!

(*The* Barman *brings the drinks,* Clitheroe *pays*)

Capt. Brennan. We won't have long to wait now.

Lieut. Langon. Th' time is rotten ripe for revolution.

Clitheroe (*to Lieut. Langon*) You have a mother, Langon.

Lieut. Langon. Ireland is greater than a mother.

Capt. Brennan (*to Clitheroe*) You have a wife, Clitheroe.

Clitheroe. Ireland is greater than a wife.

Lieut. Langon. Th' time for Ireland's battle is now—th' place for Ireland's battle is here.

(*The tall, dark figure again appears in the window. The three men stiffen to attention. They stand out from the* l *of the counter,* Brennan *nearest the counter, then* Clitheroe, *then* Lieut. Langon. Fluther *and* Rosie, *busy with each other, take no notice*)

The Voice of the Man. Our foes are strong, but strong as they are, they cannot undo the miracles of God, who ripens in the heart of young men the seeds sown by the young men of a former generation. They think they have pacified Ireland; think they have foreseen everything; think they have provided against everything; but the fools, the fools, the fools!—they have left us our Fenian dead, and, while Ireland holds these graves, Ireland, unfree, shall never be at peace!

Capt. Brennan (*lifting up the Plough and the Stars*) Imprisonment for th' Independence of Ireland!

Lieut. Langon (*lifting up the Tricolour*) Wounds for th' Independence of Ireland!

Clitheroe. Death for th' Independence of Ireland!

The Three (*together*) So help us God!

(*They lift their glasses and drink together. The 'Assembly' is heard on a bugle outside. They leave their glasses on the counter, and hurry out by the doors L.*

There is a pause. Then Fluther *and* Rosie *rise from the seat, and start to go* L. Rosie *is linking* Fluther, *who is a little drunk. Both are in a merry mood*)

Rosie. Are you afraid or what? Are you goin' to come home, or are you not?

Fluther. Of course I'm goin' home. What ud ail me that I wouldn't go?

Rosie (*lovingly*) Come on, then, oul' sport.

Officer's Voice (*giving command outside*) Irish Volunteers, by th' right, quick march!

Rosie (*putting her arm round Fluther and singing to the air 'Twenty-four Strings to my Bow'*)

I once had a lover, a tailor, but he could do nothin' for me,
An' then I fell in with a sailor as strong an' as wild as th' sea.
We cuddled an' kissed with devotion, till th' night from th'
        mornin' had fled;
An' there, to our joy, a bright bouncin' boy
Was dancin' a jig in th' bed!

Dancin' a jig in th' bed, an' bawlin' for butther an' bread.
An' there, to our joy, a bright bouncin' boy
Was dancin' a jig in th' bed!

(*They go out with their arms round each other*)

Clitheroe's Voice (*in command outside*) Dublin Battalion of the Irish Citizen Army, by th' right, quick march!

Curtain

ACT III

SCENE—*A corner house of a street of tenements; the exterior of the house in which the Clitheroes live. It is a tall, gaunt five-storey tenement. Its brick front is dull from weather and age. It juts out from L more than half-way across the stage, showing part of the front elevation, with a wide, heavy door, having windows above and on both sides. The windows on L, looking into the rooms of the Clitheroes, are hung with good casement cloth. The others are draped with grimy lace curtains. Stone steps lead from the door to the path on the street. From these steps, on each side of the door are railings to prevent anyone from falling down the area. To the extreme R the front of another house is merely indicated by the side aspect of a wall with steps leading from the door, on which the wounded Langon rests later on in the scene. Between the two runs a lane which, up stage, turns to the R. At the corner of the lane, nearest the house shown almost full front, is a street lamp.*

As the house is revealed, MRS GOGAN *is seen helping* MOLLSER *to a chair, which stands on the path beside the railings, at the L side of the steps. She then wraps a shawl around Mollser's shoulders. It is some months later.*

MRS GOGAN (*arranging the shawl around Mollser*) Th' sun'll do you all th' good in th' world. A few more weeks o' this weather, an' there's no knowin' how well you'll be . . . Are you comfy, now?

MOLLSER (*weakly and wearily*) Yis, ma; I'm all right.

MRS GOGAN (*bending over her*) How are you feelin'?

MOLLSER. Betther, ma, betther. If th' horrible sinkin' feelin' 'ud go, I'd be all right.

MRS GOGAN. Ah, I wouldn't put much pass on that. Your stomach maybe's out of ordher . . . Is th' poor breathin' any betther, d'ye think?

MOLLSER. Yis, yis, ma; a lot betther.

MRS GOGAN. Well, that's somethin' anyhow . . . With th' help o' God, you'll be on th' mend from this out . . . D'your legs feel any sthronger undher you, d'ye think?

MOLLSER (*irritably*) I can't tell, ma. I think so . . . A little.

MRS GOGAN. Well, a little aself is somethin' . . . I thought I heard you coughin' a little more than usual last night . . . D'ye think you were?

MOLLSER. I wasn't, ma, I wasn't.

MRS GOGAN. I thought I heard you, for I was kep' awake all night with th' shootin'. An' thinkin' o' that madman, Fluther,

38

runnin' about through th' night lookin' for Nora Clitheroe to bring her back when he heard she'd gone to folly her husband, an' in dhread any minute he might come staggerin' in covered with bandages, splashed all over with th' red of his own blood, an' givin' us barely time to bring th' priest to hear th' last whisper of his final confession, as his soul was passin' through th' dark doorway o' death into th' way o' th' wondherin' dead . . . You don't feel cold, do you?

MOLLSER. No, ma; I'm all right.

MRS GOGAN. Keep your chest well covered, for that's th' delicate spot in you . . . if there's any danger, I'll whip you in again . . . (*She crosses to* R, *goes up the lane, turns and looks* R, *as if looking down the street*) Oh, here's the Covey an' oul' Peter hurryin' along. (*She comes down the lane, and crosses to Mollser*) God Almighty, sthrange things is happenin' when them two is pullin' together.

(*The* COVEY *and* PETER *come into the lane* R, *come down, and stand* RC. MRS GOGAN *stands* C, *near the steps. The two men are breathless and excited*)

(*To the two men*) Were yous far up th' town? Did yous see any sign o' Fluther or Nora? How is things lookin'? I hear they're blazin' away out o' th' G.P.O. That th' Tommies is sthretched in heaps around Nelson's Pillar an' th' Parnell Statue, an' that th' pavin' sets in O'Connell Street is nearly covered be pools o' blood.

PETER. We seen no sign o' Nora or Fluther anywhere.

MRS GOGAN. We should ha' held her back be main force from goin' to look for her husband . . . God knows what's happened to her—I'm always seein' her sthretched on her back in some hospital, moanin' with th' pain of a bullet in her vitals, an' nuns thryin' to get her to take a last look at th' crucifix!

THE COVEY. We can do nothin'. You can't stick your nose into O'Connell Street, an' Tyler's is on fire.

PETER. An' we seen th' Lancers——

THE COVEY (*interrupting*) Throttin' along, heads in th' air; spurs an' sabres jinglin', an' lances quiverin', an' lookin' as if they were assin' themselves, 'Where's these blighters, till we get a prod at them,' when there was a volley from th' Post Office that stretched half o' them, an' sent th' rest gallopin' away wondherin' how far they'd have to go before they'd feel safe.

PETER (*rubbing his hands*) 'Damn it,' says I to meself, 'this looks like business!'

THE COVEY. An' then out comes General Pearse an' his staff, an', standin' in th' middle o' th' street, he reads th' Proclamation.

MRS GOGAN. What proclamation?

PETER. Declarin' an Irish Republic.

MRS GOGAN (*with amazement*) Go to God!

PETER. The gunboat *Helga's* shellin' Liberty Hall, an' I hear that people livin' on th' quays had to crawl on their bellies to Mass with th' bullets that were flyin' around from Boland's Mills.

MRS GOGAN. God bless us, what's goin' to be th' end of it all!

BESSIE (*opening and looking out of a window*) Maybe yous are satisfied now; maybe yous are satisfied now! Go on an' get guns if yous are men—Johnny get your gun, get your gun, get your gun! Yous are all nicely shanghaied now; th' boyo hasn't a sword on his thigh, now! Oh, yous are all nicely shanghaied now! (*She shuts down the window viciously*)

MRS GOGAN (*warningly to Peter and the Covey*) S-s-sh, don't answer her. She's th' right oul' Orange bitch! She's been chantin' 'Rule, Britannia' all th' mornin'.

PETER. I hope Fluther hasn't met with any accident, he's such a wild card.

THE COVEY. Fluther's well able to take care of himself.

MRS GOGAN (*dolefully*) God grant it; but last night I dreamt I seen gettin' carried into th' house a sthretcher with a figure lyin' on it, stiff an' still, dhressed in th' habit of Saint Francis. An' then, I heard th' murmurs of a crowd no one could see sayin' th' litany for th' dead; an' then it got so dark that nothin' was seen but th' white face of th' corpse, gleamin' like a white·wather lily floatin' on th' top of a dark lake. Then a tiny whisper thrickled into me ear, sayin', 'Isn't the face very like th' face o' Fluther,' an' then, with a thremblin' flutther, th' dead lips opened, an', although I couldn't hear, I knew they were sayin', 'Poor oul' Fluther, afther havin' handin' in his gun at last, his shakin' soul moored in th' place where th' wicked are at rest an' th' weary cease from throublin'.'

(*While* MRS GOGAN *is speaking,* PETER *wanders up the lane, looks* R, *then stares; then puts on his spectacles and looks again. He turns and shouts at Mrs Gogan and the Covey*)

PETER (*shouting*) Here they are, be God, here they are; just after turnin' the corner—Nora an' Fluther!

(*The* COVEY *runs up the lane and looks* R *with* PETER)

COVEY. She must be wounded or something—Fluther seems to be carryin' her.

(FLUTHER, *half carrying Nora, comes in* R; NORA'S *eyes are dim and hollow; her face pale and strained-looking; her hair is tossed and her clothes are dusty. They pass by Covey and Peter, come down the lane, and cross over to the door of the house* C. PETER *and the* COVEY *follow, and stand* R. MRS GOGAN *goes over solicitously to Nora.* NORA *wears a brown mackintosh*)

MRS GOGAN (*running over to them*) God bless us, is it wounded y'are, Mrs Clitheroe, or what?

FLUTHER (*confidently*) Ah, she's all right, Mrs Gogan; only worn out from thravellin' an' want o' sleep. A night's rest, now, an' she'll be as fit as a fiddle. Bring her in, an' make her lie down.

MRS GOGAN (to Nora) Did you hear e'er a whisper o' Mr Clitheroe?

NORA (wearily) I could find him nowhere, Mrs Gogan. None o' them would tell me where he was. They told me I shamed my husband an' th' women of Ireland be carryin' on as I was . . . They said th' women must learn to be brave an' cease to be cowardly . . . Me who risked more for love than they would risk for hate . . . (Raising her voice in hysterical protest) My Jack will be killed, my Jack will be killed! . . . He is to be butchered as a sacrifice to th' dead!

(NORA sinks down on the steps at the door. BESSIE BURGESS opens the window, and shouts at them. They do not look at her)

BESSIE. Yous are all nicely shanghaied now! Sorra mend the lassies who have been kissin' an' cuddlin' their boys into th' sheddin' of blood. Fillin' their minds with fairy tales that had no beginnin', but, please God, 'll have a bloody quick endin'! (She shuts the window with a bang)

FLUTHER (losing control) Y' ignorant oul' throllope, you!

MRS GOGAN (coaxingly, to Nora) You'll find he'll come home safe enough to you, Mrs Clitheroe. Afther all, there's a power o' women that's handed over sons an' husbands, to take a runnin' risk in th' fight they're wagin'.

NORA. I can't help thinkin' every shot fired 'll be fired at Jack, an' every shot fired at Jack 'll be fired at me. What do I care for th' others? I can think only of me own self . . . An' there's no woman gives a son or a husband to be killed—if they say it, they're lyin', lyin', against God, Nature, an' against themselves! . . . One blasted hussy at a barricade told me to go home an' not be thryin' to dishearten th' men . . .

PETER (unctuously) You'll have to have patience, Nora. We all have to put up with twarthers an' tormentors in this world.

THE COVEY. If they were fightin' for anything worth while, I wouldn't mind.

FLUTHER (to Nora) Nothin' derogatory 'll happen to Mr Clitheroe. You'll find, 'now, in th' finish up, it'll be vice versa.

NORA. Oh, I know that wherever he is, he's thinkin' of wantin' to be with me. I know he's longin' to be passin' his hand through me hair, to be caressin' me neck, to fondle me hand an' to feel me kisses clingin' to his mouth . . . An' he stands wherever he is because he's brave? (Vehemently) No, but because he's a coward, a coward, a coward!

MRS GOGAN. Oh, they're not cowards anyway.

NORA (with denunciatory anger) I tell you they're afraid to say they're afraid! . . . Oh, I saw it, I saw it, Mrs Gogan . . . At th' barricade in North King Street I saw fear glowin' in all their eyes . . . An' in th' middle o' th' sthreet was somethin' huddled up in a horrible tangled heap . . . An' I saw that they were afraid to look at it . . . I tell you they were afraid, afraid, afraid!

MRS GOGAN (*lifting her up from the steps*) Come on in, dear. If you'd been a little longer together the wrench asundher wouldn't have been so sharp.

NORA (*painfully ascending the steps, helped by Mrs Gogan*) Th' agony I'm in since he left me has thrust away every rough thing he done, an' every unkind word he spoke; only th' blossoms that grew out of our lives are before me now; shakin' their colours before me face, an' breathin' their sweet scent on every thought springin' up in me mind, till, sometimes, Mrs Gogan, sometimes I think I'm goin' mad!

MRS GOGAN. You'll be a lot betther when you have a little lie down.

NORA (*turning towards Fluther as she is going in*) I don't know what I'd have done, only for Fluther. I'd have been lyin' in th' sthreets, only for him . . . (*As she goes in*) They have dhriven away th' little happiness life had to spare for me. He has gone from me for ever, for ever . . . Oh, Jack, Jack, Jack!

(*As* NORA *is led in,* BESSIE *comes out. She passes down the steps with her head in the air; at the bottom she stops to look back. When they have gone in, she takes a mug of milk from under a shawl she is wearing and gives it to Mollser silently.* MOLLSER *takes it from her*)

FLUTHER (*going from* C *to the Covey and Peter,* R) Which of yous has the tossers?

THE COVEY. I have.

(BESSIE *crosses from Mollser to* R. *She pauses at the corner of the lane,* R, *to speak to the two men*)

BESSIE (*scornfully, to Fluther and the Covey*) You an' your Leadhers, and their sham-battle soldiers has landed a body in a nice way, havin' to go an' ferret out a bit o' bread, God knows where . . . Why aren't yous in the G.P.O., if yous are men? It's paler an' paler yous are gettin' . . . A lot of vipers—that's what the Irish people is!

(BESSIE *goes up the lane, turns* R, *and goes out*)

FLUTHER (*warningly*) Never mind her. (*To the Covey*) Make a start, an' keep us from th' sin of idleness. (*He crosses from* R *to Mollser and speaks to her*) Well, how are you today, Mollser, oul' son? What are you dhrinkin'? Milk?

MOLLSER. Grand, Fluther, grand, thanks—yes, milk.

FLUTHER (*to Mollser*) You couldn't get a betther thing down you . . . This turn-up has done one good thing, anyhow; you can't get dhrink anywhere, an' if it lasts a week I'll be so used to it that I won't think of a pint.

(FLUTHER *returns and joins the two men* R. *The* COVEY *takes from his pocket two worn coins and a thin strip of wood (or tin) about four inches long. He puts the coins on the strip of wood and holds the strip out from him*)

THE COVEY. What's the bettin'?
PETER. Heads, a juice.
FLUTHER. Harps, a tanner.

(*The* COVEY *flips the coins from the wood into the air. As they jingle on the ground the distant boom of a big gun is heard. They leave the coins where they are and listen intently*)

(*Awed*) What th' hell's that?
COVEY (*awed*) It's like the boom of a big gun?
FLUTHER. Surely to God, they're not goin' to use artillery on us!
THE COVEY (*scornfully*) Not goin'! (*Vehemently*) Wouldn't they use anything on us, man!
FLUTHER. Aw, holy Christ, that's not playin' th' game!
PETER (*plaintively*) What would happen if a shell landed here now?
THE COVEY (*ironically*) You'd be off to heaven in a ficry chariot.
PETER. In spite of all th' warnin's that's ringin' around us, are you goin' to start your pickin' at me again?
FLUTHER. Go on, toss them again, toss them again . . . Harps, a tanner.
PETER. Heads, a juice.

(*The* COVEY *tosses the coins as before; they fall on the ground and roll a little.* FLUTHER *waves the other two back as they bend over the rolling coins*)

FLUTHER. Let them roll, let them roll—heads be God!

(BESSIE *runs in* R, *runs down the lane towards the three men. She is breathless with excitement. She has a new fox fur round her neck over her shawl, a number of new umbrellas under one arm, a box of biscuits under the other, and she wears a gaudily trimmed hat on her head. She speaks rapidly and breathlessly*)

BESSIE. They're breakin' into th' shops, they're breakin' into th' shops! Smashin' th' windows, batterin' in th' doors an' whippin' away everything! An' th' Volunteers is firin' on them. I seen two men an' a lassie pushin' a piano down th' sthreet, an' th' sweat rollin' off them thryin' to get it up on th' pavement; an' an oul' wan that must ha' been seventy lookin' as if she'd dhrop every minute with th' dint o' heart beatin', thryin' to pull a big double bed out of a broken shop window! I was goin' to wait till I dhressed meself from th' skin out.
MOLLSER (*to* BESSIE, *as she is going into the house* C) Help me in, Bessie; I'm feelin' curious.

(BESSIE *leaves the looted things in the house, and, rapidly returning, helps Mollser in*)

THE COVEY (*to Fluther*) Th' selfishness of that one—she waited till she got all she could carry before she'd come to tell anyone! FLUTHER (*running over to the door of the house and shouting in to Bessie*) Ay, Bessie, did you hear of e'er a pub gettin' a shake up? BESSIE (*inside*) I didn't hear o' none. FLUTHER (*in a burst of enthusiasm*) Well, you're goin' to hear of one soon! THE COVEY (*to Fluther, excitedly*) Come on, man, an' don't be wastin' time. PETER (*calling to them as they run up the lane*) E, eh, are yous goin' to leave me here, alone?

(FLUTHER *and* COVEY *halt in the middle of the lane, and turn to look and reply to Peter*)

FLUTHER. Are you goin' to leave yourself here? PETER (*anxiously*) Didn't yous hear her sayin' they were firin' on them? THE COVEY *and* FLUTHER (*together*) Well? PETER. Supposin' I happened to be potted? FLUTHER. We'd give you a Christian burial, anyhow. THE COVEY (*ironically*) Dhressed up in your regimentals. PETER (*to the Covey, passionately*) May th' all-lovin' God give you a hot knock one o' these days, me young Covey, tuthorin' Fluther up now to be tiltin' at me, an' crossin' me with his mockeries an' jibin'!

(FLUTHER *and* COVEY *run up the lane, and go off* R. PETER *looks after them and then goes slowly into the house* C.

After a slight pause, MRS GOGAN *appears at the door of the house* C, *pushing a pram in front of her. As she gets the pram over the threshold* BESSIE *appears, catches the pram, and stops Mrs Gogan's progress*)

BESSIE (*angrily*) Here, where are you goin' with that? How quick you were, me lady, to clap your eyes on th' pram . . . Maybe you don't know that Mrs Sullivan, before she went to spend Easther with her people in Dunboyne, gave me sthrict injunctions to give an occasional look to see if it was still standin' where it was left in th' corner of th' lobby. MRS GOGAN (*indignantly*) That remark of yours, Mrs Bessie Burgess, requires a little considheration, seein' that th' pram was left on our lobby, an' not on yours; a foot or two a little to th' left of th' jamb of me own room door; nor is it needful to mention th' name of th' person that gave a squint to see if it was there th' first thing in th' mornin', an' th' last thing in th' stillness o' th' night; never failin' to realize that her eyes couldn't be goin' wrong, be sthretchin' out her arm an' runnin' her hand over th' pram, to make sure that th' sight was no deception! Moreover, somethin's tellin' me that th' runnin' hurry of an inthrest you're takin' in it now is a sudden ambition to use th' pram for a purpose, that a loyal woman of law an' ordher would stagger away from!

(MRS GOGAN *pushes the pram violently down the steps, pulling* BESSIE *with her, who holds her up again when they reach the street*)

BESSIE (*still holding the pram*) There's not as much as one body in th' house that doesn't know that it wasn't Bessie Burgess that was always shakin' her voice complainin' about people leavin' bassinettes in th' way of them that, week in an' week out, had to pay their rent, an' always had to find a regular accommodation for her own furniture in her own room . . . An' as for law an' ordher, puttin' aside th' harp an' shamrock, Bessie Burgess 'll have as much respect as she wants for th' lion an' unicorn!

PETER (*appearing at the door of the house* C) I think I'll go with th' pair of yous an' see th' fun. A fella might as well chance it, anyhow.

MRS GOGAN (*taking no notice of Peter, and pushing the pram on towards the lane*) Take your rovin' lumps o' hands from pattin' th' bassinette, if you please, ma'am; an', steppin' from th' threshold of good manners, let me tell you, Mrs Burgess, that it's a fat wondher to Jennie Gogan that a lady-like singer o' hymns like yourself would lower her thoughts from sky-thinkin' to sthretch out her arm in a sly-seekin' way to pinch anything dhriven asthray in th' confusion of th' battle our boys is makin' for th' freedom of their counthry!

PETER (*laughing and rubbing his hands together*) Hee, hee, hee, hee, hee! I'll go with th' pair o' yous an' give yous a hand.

MRS GOGAN (*with a rapid turn of her head as she shoves the pram forward*) Get up in th' prambulator an' we'll wheel you down.

BESSIE (*to Mrs Gogan as she halts the pram again*) Poverty an' hardship has sent Bessie Burgess to abide with sthrange company, but she always knew them she had to live with from backside to breakfast time; an' she can tell them, always havin' had a Christian kinch on her conscience, that a passion for thievin' an' pinchin' would find her soul a foreign place to live in, an' that her present intention is quite th' lofty-hearted one of pickin' up anything shaken up an' scatthered about in th' loose confusion of a general plundher!

(MRS GOGAN, BESSIE *and the pram run up the lane and go off* R. PETER *follows, but as he reaches the corner of the lane the boom of the big gun brings him to a sudden halt*)

PETER (*frightened into staying behind by the sound of the gun*) God Almighty, that's th' big gun again! God forbid any harm would

happen to them, but sorra mind I'd mind if they met with a dhrop
in their mad endeyvours to plundher an' desthroy.

(PETER *looks down the street from the lane for a moment, then runs
to the hall door of the house* c, *which is open, and shuts it with a vicious
pull; he then goes to the chair in which Mollser had sat, sits down,
takes out his pipe, lights it and begins to smoke with his head carried
at a haughty angle.*

The COVEY *comes in* R *and down the lane, staggering with a ten-
stone sack of flour on his back. He goes over to the door, pushes it with his
head, and finds he can't open it; he turns slightly in the direction of Peter*)

THE COVEY (*to Peter*) Who shut th' door? . . . (*He kicks at it*)
Here, come on an' open it, will you? This isn't a mot's hand-bag
I've got on me back.

PETER. Now, me young Covey, d'ye think I'm goin' to be your
lackey?

THE COVEY (*angrily*) Will you open th' door, y'oul'——

PETER (*shouting*) Don't be assin' me to open any door, don't be
assin' me to open any door for you . . . Makin' a shame an' a sin
o' th' cause that good men are fightin' for . . . Oh, God forgive
th' people that, instead o' burnishin' th' work th' boys is doin'
today, with quiet honesty an' patience, is revilin' their sacrifices
with a riot of lootin' an' roguery!

THE COVEY (*sarcastically*) Isn't your own eyes leppin' out o' your
head with envy that you haven't th' guts to ketch a few o' th'
things that God is givin' to His chosen people? . . . Y'oul' hypo-
crite, if everyone was blind you'd steal a cross off an ass's back!

PETER (*very calmly*) You're not goin' to make me lose me temper; you can go on with your proddin' as long as you like; goad
an' goad an' goad away; hee hee, heee! I'll not lose me temper.

(*Somebody opens the door and the* COVEY *goes in*)

THE COVEY (*inside the house, to mock Peter*) Cuckoo-oo!

(PETER *gets up from the chair in a blaze of passion, and follows the
Covey in, shouting*)

PETER (*shouting*) You lean, long, lanky lath of a lowsey bastard.
(*Going in the door of the house,* c) Lowsey bastard, lowsey bastard!

(MRS GOGAN *and* BESSIE, *pushing the pram, come in* R, *come down
the lane to the front of the house* c. BESSIE *is pushing the pram, which
is filled with loot.* MRS GOGAN *carries a tall standard lamp, topped
with a wide and bright-coloured shade. The pram is filled with fancy-
coloured dresses, and boots and shoes. They are talking as they
appear* R)

MRS GOGAN (*appearing* R) I don't remember ever havin' seen
such lovely pairs as them with the pointed toes an' the cuban
heels.

BESSIE (*they are now* C, *lifting one of the evening-dresses from the pram, holding it up admiringly*) They'll go grand with th' dhresses we're afther liftin', when we've stitched a sthray bit o' silk to lift th' bodices up a little bit higher, so as to shake th' shame out o' them, an' make them fit for women that hasn't lost themselves in th' nakedness o' th' times.

PETER (*at the door, sourly to Mrs Gogan*) Ay, you. Mollser looks as if she was goin' to faint, an' your youngster is roarin' in convulsions in her lap.

MRS GOGAN (*snappily*) She's never any other way but faintin'!

(MRS GOGAN *runs into the house with her arm full of things. She comes back, takes up the lamp and is about to go in, when a rifle-shot very near is heard.* MRS GOGAN, *with the lamp, and* BESSIE, *with the pram, rush to the door which* PETER, *in a panic, has shut*)

(*Banging at the door*) Eh, eh, you cowardly oul' fool, what are you thryin' to shut the door on us for?

(MRS GOGAN *pushes the door open and runs in, followed by* BESSIE *dragging in the pram. They shut the door.*
There is a pause. Then CAPT. BRENNAN, *supporting* LIEUT. LANGON, *comes in* L, *along the street in front of the house* C. *As* BRENNAN *and* LANGON *reach* C *going* R, CLITHEROE, *pale and in a state of calm nervousness, appears at* L, *walking backwards or looking back in the direction from which they've come ; he has a rifle held at the ready in his hands.* LANGON *is ghastly white and now and again his face is twisted in agony*)

CAPT. BRENNAN (*back to Clitheroe*) Why did you fire over their heads? Why didn't you fire to kill?

CLITHEROE. No, no, Bill; bad as they are, they're Irish men an' women.

(BRENNAN *gently lets* LANGON *recline on the steps of the house indicated to the extreme* R, *holding him by an arm.* CLITHEROE *is* C, *watching Langon*)

CAPT. BRENNAN (*savagely*) Irish be damned! Attackin' an' mobbin' th' men that are riskin' their lives for them. If these slum lice gather at our heels again, plug one o' them, or I'll soon shock them with a shot or two meself!

LIEUT. LANGON (*moaningly*) My God, is there ne'er an ambulance knockin' around anywhere? . . . Th' stomach is ripped out o' me; I feel it—o-o-oh, Christ!

CAPT. BRENNAN. Keep th' heart up, Jim; we'll soon get help, now.

(*The door of the house* C *opens and* NORA *rushes out, and dashes down the steps into* CLITHEROE'S *arms at the bottom. She flings her arms around his neck. Her hair is down, her face haggard, but her eyes are agleam with happy relief*)

NORA (*to Clitheroe*) Jack, Jack, oh, God be thanked. Kiss me, kiss me, Jack; kiss your own Nora.

CLITHEROE (*kissing her, and speaking brokenly*) My Nora; my little, beautiful Nora, I wish to God I'd never left you.

NORA. It doesn't matter—not now, not now, Jack. It will make us dearer than ever to each other . . . Kiss me, kiss me again.

CLITHEROE. Now, for God's sake, Nora, don't make a scene.

NORA (*fervently*) I won't, I won't; I promise, Jack—honest to God.

(BESSIE *opens the window of house to the* R, *puts out her head, and shouts at Clitheroe and Brennan*)

BESSIE (*at the window*) Has th' big guns knocked all th' harps out of your hands? General Clitheroe'd rather be unlacin' his wife's bodice now, than standin' at a barricade. (*To Brennan*) An' the professor of chicken butcherin', there, finds he's up against something a little tougher than his own chickens, an' that's sayin' a lot!

CAPT. BRENNAN (*over to Bessie*) Shut up, y'oul' hag!

BESSIE (*down to Brennan*) Choke th' chicken, choke th' chicken, choke th' chicken!

LIEUT. LANGON. For God's sake, Bill, bring me some place where me wound 'll be looked afther . . . Am I to die before anything is done to save me?

CAPT. BRENNAN (*to Clitheroe*) Come on, Jack. We've got to get help for Jim, here—have you no thought for his pain an' danger?

BESSIE. Choke th' chicken, choke th' chicken, choke th' chicken!

CLITHEROE (*to Nora*) Loosen me, darling, let me go.

NORA (*clinging to him*) No, no, no, I'll not let you go! Come on, come up to our home, Jack, my sweetheart, my lover, my husband, an' we'll forget th' last few terrible days! . . .

LIEUT. LANGON (*appealingly*) Oh, if I'd kep' down only a little longer, I mightn't ha' been hit! Everyone else escapin', an' me gettin' me belly ripped asundher! . . . I couldn't scream, couldn't even scream . . . D'ye think I'm really badly wounded, Bill? Me clothes seem to be all soakin' wet . . . It's blood . . . My God, it must be me own blood!

CAPT. BRENNAN (*to Clitheroe*) Go on, Jack, bid her good-bye with another kiss, an' be done with it! D'ye want Langon to die in me arms while you're dallyin' with your Nora?

CLITHEROE (*to Nora*) I must go, I must go, Nora, I'm sorry we met at all . . . It couldn't be helped—all other ways were blocked be th' British . . . Let me go, can't you, Nora? D'ye want me to be unthrue to me comrades?

NORA. No, I won't let you go . . . I want you to be thrue to me, Jack . . . I'm your dearest comrade; I'm your thruest comrade. (*Tightening her arms round Clitheroe*) Oh, Jack, I can't let you go!

CLITHEROE (*with anger, mixed with affection*) You must, Nora, you must.

NORA. All last night at the barricades I sought you, Jack. I asked for you everywhere. I didn't think of the danger—I could only think of you. They dhrove me away, but I came back again.

CLITHEROE (*ashamed of her action*) What possessed you to make a show of yourself, like that! What are you more than any other woman?

NORA. No more, maybe; but you are more to me than any other man, Jack . . . I couldn't help it . . . I shouldn't have told you . . . My love for you made me mad with terror.

CLITHEROE (*angrily*) They'll say now that I sent you out th' way I'd have an excuse to bring you home . . . Are you goin' to turn all th' risks I'm takin' into a laugh?

LIEUT. LANGON. Let me lie down, let me lie down, Bill; th' pain would be easier, maybe, lyin' down . . . Oh, God, have mercy on me!

CAPT. BRENNAN (*encouragingly to Langon*) A few steps more, Jim, a few steps more; thry to stick it for a few steps more.

LIEUT. LANGON. Oh, I can't, I can't, I can't!

CAPT. BRENNAN (*to Clitheroe*) Are you comin', man, or are you goin' to make an arrangement for another honeymoon? . . . If you want to act th' renegade, say so, an' we'll be off!

BESSIE (*from the window*) Runnin' from th' Tommies—choke th' chicken. Runnin' from th' Tommies—choke th' chicken!

CLITHEROE (*savagely to Brennan*) Damn you, man, who wants to act th' renegade? (*To Nora*) Here, let go your hold; let go, I say!

NORA (*clinging to Clitheroe, and indicating Brennan*) Look, Jack, look at th' anger in his face; look at th' fear glintin' in his eyes . . . He, himself's afraid, afraid, afraid! . . . He wants you to go th' way he'll have th' chance of death sthrikin' you an' missin' him! . . .

CLITHEROE (*struggling to release himself from Nora*) Damn you, woman, will you let me go!

CAPT. BRENNAN (*fiercely, to Clitheroe*) Break her hold on you, man; or go up an' sit on her lap!

(CLITHEROE *tries to break her hold with his right hand (he's holding his rifle in the other), but* NORA *clings to him*)

NORA (*imploringly*) Jack, Jack, Jack!

LIEUT. LANGON (*agonizingly*) Brennan, a priest; I'm dyin', I think. I'm dyin'.

CLITHEROE (*to Nora*) If you won't do it quietly, I'll have to make you! (*To Brennan*) Here, hold this gun, you, for a minute. (*He hands the gun to Brennan*)

NORA (*pitifully*) Please, Jack . . . You're hurting me, Jack . . . Honestly . . . Oh, you're hurting . . . me! . . . I won't, I won't,

I won't! . . . Oh, Jack, I gave you everything you asked of me
. . . Don't fling me from you, now!

(CLITHEROE *roughly loosens her grip, and pushes her away from him.*
NORA *sinks to the steps at the door, and lies there*)

(*Weakly*) Ah, Jack . . . Jack . . . Jack!
CLITHEROE (*taking the gun back from Brennan*) Come on, come
on.

(CLITHEROE *hurries over to Brennan, and catches hold of Langon's
other arm; they both lift him up from the steps, and supporting him,
turn into the lane and go off* R.

BESSIE *looks at Nora lying on the street, for a few moments, then,
leaving the window, she comes out, runs over to Nora, lifts her up in
her arms, and carries her swiftly into the house.*

*There is a short pause, then down the street is heard a wild,
drunken yell; it comes nearer, and* FLUTHER *enters, frenzied, wild-
eyed, mad, roaring drunk. In his arms is an earthen half-gallon jar of
whiskey; streaming from one of the pockets of his coat is the arm of a
new tunic shirt; on his head is a woman's vivid blue hat with gold
lacing, all of which he has looted.*

The evening begins to darken)

FLUTHER (*singing in a frenzy, as he comes down the lane*) Fluther's
        a jolly good fella . . .
    Fluther's a jolly good fella . . . up th' rebels!
    . . . that nobody can deny!

(*He reels across to* L, *staggers up the steps of the house* C, *and hammers
at the door*) Get us a mug, or a jug, or somethin', some o' yous,
one o' yous, will yous, before I lay one o' yous out!

(*Rifle firing is heard some distance away and the boom of the big gun.*
FLUTHER *turns from the door, and looks off* R)

Bang an' fire away for all Fluther cares. (*He beats at the door*)
Come down an' open th' door, some o' yous, one o' yous, will
yous, before I lay some o' yous out! . . . Th' whole city can
topple home to hell, for Fluther.

(*Inside the house* C *is heard a scream from* NORA, *followed by a
moan*)

(*Singing frantically*) That nobody can deny, that nobody can deny,
        For Fluther's a jolly good fella,
        Fluther's a jolly good fella,
        Fluther's a jolly good fella . . . up th' rebels!
        . . . that nobody can deny!

(FLUTHER'S *frantic movements cause him to spill some of the
whiskey out of the jar*)

(*Looking down at the jar*) Blast you, Fluther, don't be spillin' th' precious liquor! (*He kicks at the door*) Give us a mug, or a jug, or somethin', one o' yous, some o' yous, will yous, before I lay one o' yous out!

(*The door suddenly opens, and* BESSIE, *coming out, grips him by the collar*)

BESSIE (*indignantly*) You bowsey, come in ower o' that . . . I'll thrim your thricks o' dhrunken dancin' for you, an' none of us knowin' how soon we'll bump into a world we were never in before!

FLUTHER (*as she is pulling him in*) Ay, th' jar, th' jar, th' jar. *Mind th' jar!*

(*A short pause, then again is heard a scream of pain from* NORA. *The door opens and* MRS GOGAN *and* BESSIE *are seen standing at it. The light gets dim*)

BESSIE. Fluther would go, only he's too dhrunk . . . Oh, God, isn't it a pity he's so dhrunk! We'll have to thry to get a docthor somewhere.

MRS GOGAN. I'd be afraid to go . . . Besides, Mollser's terrible bad. I don't think you'll get a docthor to come. It's hardly any use goin'.

BESSIE (*determinedly*) I'll risk it . . . Give her a little of Fluther's whiskey . . . It's th' fright that's brought it on her so soon . . . Go on back to her, you.

(MRS GOGAN *goes into the house, and* BESSIE *softly closes the door. She comes down the steps, and is half-way across to* R, *when rifle-firing and the tok-tok-tok of a machine-gun bring her to a sudden halt. She hesitates for a moment, then tightens her shawl round her, as if it were a shield*)

(*Softly*) O God, be Thou my help in time o' throuble; an' shelther me safely in th' shadow of Thy wings.

(BESSIE *goes forward, goes up the lane, and goes off* R)

CURTAIN

ACT IV

SCENE—*The living-room of Bessie Burgess. It is one of two small attic rooms (the other, used as a bedroom, is on the* L*), the low ceiling slopes down towards the back. There is an unmistakable air of poverty about the room. The paper on the walls is torn and soiled. On the* R*, down stage, is a door. There is a small window* C *back. To* L *of the window is a well-worn dresser, with a small quantity of Delft. On the* L *wall, up stage, is a door leading to a bedroom. The door on* R *leads to the rest of the house and street. Below the door on the* L *wall, the fireplace. Inside the fender is a kettle and saucepan. On the hob a teapot. In front of the fire a well-worn armchair. In front of the window, back, a little to the* R*, an oak coffin stands on two kitchen chairs. On the floor, in front of the coffin, is a wooden box, on which are two lighted candles in candlesticks. In front of the coffin, a little to* L*, a small kitchen table. At the* R *end of the table, a kitchen chair. In the corner where* R *and back walls meet, the standard lamp, with coloured shade, looted in Act II, stands; beside the lamp, hanging from the nail in the wall, back, hangs one of the evening-dresses. There is no light in the room but that given from the two candles and the fire. The dusk has well fallen, and the glare of the burning buildings in the town can be seen through the windows in the distant sky. The Covey, Fluther and Peter have been playing cards, sitting on the floor by the light of the candles on the box near the coffin.*

When the CURTAIN *rises the* COVEY *is shuffling the cards,* PETER *is sitting in a stiff, dignified way opposite him, and* FLUTHER *is kneeling beside the window, back, cautiously looking out into the street. It is a few days later.*

FLUTHER (*furtively peeping out of the window*) Give them a good shuffling . . . Th' sky's gettin' reddher an' reddher . . . You'd think it was afire . . . Half o' th' city must be burnin'.

THE COVEY (*warningly*) If I was you, Fluther, I'd keep away from that window . . . It's dangerous, an', besides, if they see you, you'll only bring a nose on th' house.

PETER (*anxiously*) Yes; an' he knows we had to leave our own place th' way they were riddlin' it with machine-gun fire . . . He'll keep on pimpin' an' pimpin' there, till we have to fly out o' this place too.

FLUTHER (*ironically to Peter*) If they make any attack here, we'll send you out in your green an' glory uniform, shakin' your sword over your head, an' they'll fly before you as th' Danes flew before Brian Boru!

THE COVEY (*placing the cards on the floor, after shuffling them*) Come on, an' cut.

(FLUTHER *creeps,* L *end of the table, over to where Covey and Peter are seated, and squats down on the floor between them*)
(*Having dealt the cards*) Spuds up again.

(NORA *moans feebly in the room on* L. *They listen for a moment*)

FLUTHER. There, she's at it again. She's been quiet for a good long time, all th' same.

THE COVEY. She was quiet before, sure, an' she broke out again worse than ever . . . What was led that time?

PETER (*Impatiently*) Thray o' Hearts, Thray o' Hearts, Thray o' Hearts.

FLUTHER. It's damned hard lines to think of her dead-born kiddie lyin' there in th' arms o' poor little Mollser. Mollser snuffed it, sudden too, afther all.

THE COVEY. Sure she never got any care. How could she get it, an' th' mother out day an' night lookin' for work, an' her consumptive husband leavin' her with a baby to be born before he died.

VOICES (*in a lilting chant to the* L *in an outside street*) Red Cr . . . oss, Red Cr . . . oss! . . . Ambu . . . lance, Ambu . . . lance!

THE COVEY (*to Fluther*) Your deal, Fluther.

FLUTHER (*shuffling and dealing the cards*) It'll take a lot out o' Nora—if she'll ever be th' same.

THE COVEY. Th' docthor thinks she'll never be th' same; thinks she'll be a little touched here. (*He touches his forehead*) She's ramblin' a lot; thinkin' she's out in th' counthry with Jack; or, gettin' his dinner ready for him before he comes home; or, yellin' for her kiddie. All that, though, might be th' chloroform she got . . . I don't know what we'd have done only for oul' Bessie: up with her for th' past three nights, hand runnin'.

FLUTHER (*approvingly*) I always knew there was never anything really derogatory wrong with poor Bessie. (*Suddenly catching Peter's arm as he is taking a trick*) Eh, houl' on there, don't be so damn quick—that's my thrick!

PETER (*resentfully*) What's your thrick? It's my thrick, man.

FLUTHER (*loudly*) How is it your thrick?

PETER (*answering as loudly*) Didn't I lead th' deuce!

FLUTHER. You must be gettin' blind, man; don't you see th' ace?

BESSIE (*appearing at the door of the room,* L; *in a tense whisper*) D'ye want to waken her again on me, when she's just gone asleep? If she wakes will yous come an' mind her? If I hear a whisper out o' one o' yous again, I'll . . . gut yous!

THE COVEY (*in a whisper*) S-s-sh. She can hear anything above a whisper.

PETER (*looking up at the ceiling*) Th' gentle an' merciful God 'll give th' pair o' yous a scawldin' an' a scarifyin' one o' these days!

(FLUTHER *takes a bottle of whiskey from his pocket, and takes a drink*)

THE COVEY (*to Fluther*) Why don't you spread that out, man, an' thry to keep a sup for tomorrow?
FLUTHER. Spread it out? Keep a sup for tomorrow? How th' hell does a fella know there'll be any tomorrow? If I'm goin' to be whipped away, let me be whipped away when it's empty, an' not when it's half-full!

(BESSIE *comes in a tired way from the door of the room* L, *down to the armchair by the fire, and sits down*)

(*Over to Bessie*) Well, how is she now, Bessie?
BESSIE. I left her sleeping quietly. When I'm listenin' to her babblin', I think she'll never be much betther than she is. Her eyes have a hauntin' way of lookin' in instead of lookin' out, as if her mind had been lost alive in madly minglin' memories of th' past . . . (*Sleepily*) Crushin' her thoughts . . . together . . . in a fierce . . . an' fanciful . . . (*she nods her head and starts wakefully*) idea that dead things are livin', an' livin' things are dead . . . (*With a start*) Was that a scream I heard her give? (*Reassured*) Blessed God, I think I hear her screamin' every minute! An' it's only there with me that I'm able to keep awake.
THE COVEY. She'll sleep, maybe, for a long time, now. Ten here.
FLUTHER (*gathering up the cards*) Ten here. If she gets a long sleep, she might be all right. Peter's th' lone five.
THE COVEY (*suddenly*) Whisht! I think I hear somebody movin' below. Whoever it is, he's comin' up.

(*There is a pause. Then the door* R *opens, and* CAPT. BRENNAN *comes timidly in. He has changed his uniform for a suit of civvies. His eyes droop with the heaviness of exhaustion; his face is pallid and drawn. His clothes are dusty and stained here and there with mud. He leans heavily on the back of a chair at the* R *end of the table*)

CAPT. BRENNAN. Mrs Clitheroe; where's Mrs Clitheroe? I was told I'd find her here.
BESSIE. What d'ye want with Mrs Clitheroe?
CAPT. BRENNAN. I've a message, a last message for her from her husband.
BESSIE. Killed! He's not killed, is he!
CAPT. BRENNAN (*sinking stiffly and painfully on to a chair*) In th' Imperial Hotel; we fought till th' place was in flames. He was shot through th' arm, an' then through th' lung . . . I could do nothin' for him—only watch his breath comin' an' goin' in quick, jerky gasps, an' a tiny sthream o' blood thricklin' out of his mouth down over his lower lip . . . I said a prayer for th' dyin', an' twined his Rosary beads around his fingers . . . Then I had to

leave him to save meself . . . (*He shows some holes in his coat*) Look at th' way a machine-gun tore at me coat, as I belted out o' th' buildin' an' darted across th' sthreet for shelter . . . An' then, I seen The Plough an' th' Stars fallin' like a shot as th' roof crashed in, an' where I'd left poor Jack was nothin' but a leppin' spout o' flame!

BESSIE (*with partly repressed vehemence*) Ay, you left him! You twined his Rosary beads round his fingers, an' then, you run like a hare to get out o' danger!

CAPT. BRENNAN (*defensively*) I took me chance as well as him . . . He took it like a man. His last whisper was to 'Tell Nora to be brave; that I'm ready to meet my God, an' that I'm proud to die for Ireland.' An' when our General heard it he said that 'Commandant Clitheroe's end was a gleam of glory.' Mrs Clitheroe's grief will be a joy when she realizes that she has had a hero for a husband.

BESSIE. If you only seen her, you'd know to th' differ.

(NORA *appears at the door,* L. *She is clad only in her nightdress and slippers; her hair, uncared for some days, is hanging in disorder over her shoulders. Her pale face looks paler still because of a vivid red spot on the tip of each cheek. Her eyes are glimmering with the light of incipient insanity; her hands are nervously fiddling with her nightgown. She halts at the door for a moment, looks vacantly around the room, and then comes slowly in. The rest do not notice her till she speaks.* BESSIE *has fallen asleep in chair.*

PETER, COVEY *and* FLUTHER *stop their card-playing and watch her*)

NORA (*roaming slowly towards* R *to back of the table*) No . . . not there, Jack . . . I feel very, very tired . . . (*Passing her hand across her eyes*) Curious mist on my eyes. Why don't you hold my hand, Jack . . . (*Excitedly*) No, no, Jack, it's not: can't you see it's a goldfinch? Look at the black satiny wings, with the gold bars, an' th' splash of crimson on its head . . . (*Wearily*) Something ails me, something ails me . . . (*Frightened*) You're goin' away, an' I can't follow you! (*She wanders back to the* L *end of the table*) I can't follow you. (*Crying out*) Jack, Jack, Jack!

(BESSIE *wakes with a start, sees* NORA, *gets up and runs to her*)

BESSIE (*putting her arm round Nora*) Mrs Clitheroe, aren't you a terrible woman to get up out o' bed . . . You'll get cold if you stay here in them clothes.

NORA (*monotonously*) Cold? I'm feelin' very cold . . . it's chilly out here in th' counthry. (*Looking around, frightened*) What place is this? Where am I?

BESSIE (*coaxingly*) You're all right, Nora; you're with friends, an' in a safe place. Don't you know your uncle an' your cousin, an' poor oul' Fluther?

PETER (*rising to go over to Nora*) Nora, darlin', now——
FLUTHER (*pulling him back*) Now, leave her to Bessie, man. A crowd 'll only make her worse.
NORA (*thoughtfully*) There is something I want to remember, an' I can't. (*With agony*) I can't, I can't, I can't! My head, my head! (*Suddenly breaking from Bessie, and running over to the men, and gripping Fluther by the shoulders*) Where is it? Where's my baby? Tell me where you've put it, where've you hidden it? My baby, my baby; I want my baby! My head, my poor head . . . Oh, I can't tell what is wrong with me. (*Screaming*) Give him to me, give me my husband!
BESSIE. Blessin' o' God on us, isn't this pitiful!
NORA (*struggling with Bessie*) I won't go away for you; I won't. Not till you give me back my husband. (*Screaming*) Murderers, that's what yous are; murderers, murderers!

(BESSIE *gently, but firmly, pulls her from Fluther, and tries to lead her to her room,* L)

BESSIE (*tenderly*) S-s-sh. We'll bring Mr Clitheroe back to you, if you'll only lie down an' stop quiet . . . (*Trying to lead her in*) Come on, now, Nora, an' I'll sing something to you.
NORA. I feel as if my life was thryin' to force its way out of my body . . . I can hardly breathe . . . I'm frightened, I'm frightened, I'm frightened! For God's sake, don't leave me, Bessie. Hold my hand, put your arms around me!
FLUTHER (*to Brennan*) Now you can see th' way she is, man.
PETER. An' what way would she be if she heard Jack had gone west?
THE COVEY (*to Peter, warningly*) Shut up, you, man!
BESSIE (*to Nora*) We'll have to be brave, an' let patience clip away th' heaviness of th' slow-movin' hours, rememberin' that sorrow may endure for th' night, but joy cometh in th' mornin' . . . Come on in, an' I'll sing to you, an' you'll rest quietly.
NORA (*stopping suddenly on her way to the room*) Jack an' me are goin' out somewhere this evenin'. Where I can't tell. Isn't it curious I can't remember . . . (*Screaming, and pointing* R) He's there, he's there, an' they won't give him back to me!
BESSIE. S-ss-s-h, darlin', s-ssh. I won't sing to you, if you're not quiet.
NORA (*nervously holding Bessie*) Hold my hand, hold my hand, an' sing to me, sing to me!
BESSIE. Come in an' lie down, an' I'll sing to you.
NORA (*vehemently*) Sing to me, sing to me; sing, sing!
BESSIE (*singing as she leads Nora into the room,* L) Lead, kindly light,
            amid th' encircling gloom,
      Lead Thou me on.
   Th' night is dark an' I am far from home,
      Lead Thou me on.

(*Leading Nora*, BESSIE *goes into the room*, L)

(*Singing softly inside the room*, L)
    Keep thou my feet, I do not ask to see
    Th' distant scene—one step enough for me.

THE COVEY (*to Brennan*) Now that you've seen how bad she is, an' that we daren't tell her what has happened till she's betther, you'd best be slippin' back to where you come from.

CAPT. BRENNAN. There's no chance o' slippin' back now, for th' military are everywhere: a fly couldn't get through. I'd never have got here, only I managed to change me uniform for what I'm wearin' . . . I'll have to take me chance, an' thry to lie low here for a while.

THE COVEY (*frightened*) There's no place here to lie low. Th' Tommies 'll be hoppin' in here, any minute!

PETER (*aghast*) An' then we'd all be shanghaied!

THE COVEY. Be God, there's enough afther happenin' to us!

FLUTHER (*warningly, as he listens*) Whisht, whisht, th' whole o' yous. I think I heard th' clang of a rifle butt on th' floor of th' hall below. (*All alertness*) Here, come on with th' cards again. I'll deal. (*He shuffles and deals the cards to all*) Clubs up. (*To Brennan*) Thry to keep your hands from shakin', man. You lead, Peter. (*As* PETER *throws out a card*) Four o' Hearts led.

(*Heavy steps are heard coming up the stairs, outside the door* R. *The door opens and* CORPORAL STODDART *of the Wiltshires enters in full war kit—steel helmet, rifle, bayonet and trench tools. He stands near the door* R, *looks around the room, and at the men who go on silently playing cards. There is a pause*)

(*Gathering up the cards, and breaking the silence*) Two tens an' a five.

CORPORAL STODDART. 'Ello. (*Indicating the coffin*) This the stiff?

THE COVEY. Yis.

CORPORAL STODDART. Who's gowing with it? Ownly one allowed to gow with it, you knaow.

THE COVEY. I dunno.

CORPORAL STODDART. You dunnow?

THE COVEY. I dunno.

BESSIE (*coming into the room*) She's afther slippin' off to sleep again, thanks be to God. I'm hardly able to keep me own eyes open. (*To the soldier*) Oh, are yous goin' to take away poor little Mollser?

CORPORAL STODDART. Ay; 'oo's agowing with 'er?

BESSIE. Oh, th' poor mother, o' course. God help her, it's a terrible blow to her!

FLUTHER. A terrible blow? Sure, she's in her element now, woman, mixin' earth to earth, an' ashes t'ashes, an' dust to dust, an' revellin' in plumes an' hearses, last days an' judgements!

BESSIE (*falling into the chair by the fire*) God bless us! I'm jaded!

CORPORAL STODDART. Was she plugged?

THE COVEY. No; died of consumption.

CORPORAL STODDART (*carelessly*) Ow, is that all—thought she might 'ave been plugged.

THE COVEY (*indignantly*) Is that all! Isn't it enough? D'ye know, comrade, that more die o' consumption than are killed in the war? An' it's all because of th' system we're livin' undher.

CORPORAL STODDART. Ow, I know. I'm a Socialist, myself, but I 'as to do my dooty.

THE COVEY (*ironically*) Dooty! Th' only dooty of a Socialist is th' emancipation of th' workers.

CORPORAL STODDART. Ow, a man's a man, an' 'e 'as to fight for 'is country, 'asn't 'e?

FLUTHER (*aggressively*) You're not fightin' for your counthry here, are you?

PETER (*anxiously, to Fluther*) Ay, ay, Fluther, none o' that, none o' that!

THE COVEY. Fight for your counthry! Did y'ever read, comrade, Jenersky's *Thesis on the Origin, Development an' Consolidation of th' Evolutionary Idea of the Prolitariat?*

CORPORAL STODDART (*good-humouredly*) Ow, cheese it, Paddy, cheese it!

BESSIE (*sleepily*) How is things in th' town, Tommy?

CORPORAL STODDART. Ow, I think it's nearly over. We've got 'em surrounded, an' we're closing in on the blighters. It was only a bit of a dorg-fight.

(*Outside in the street is heard the sharp ping of a sniper's rifle, followed by a squeal of pain*)

VOICES (*to the L in a chant, outside in the street*) Red Cr . . . oss, Red Cr . . . oss! Ambu . . . lance, Ambu . . . lance!

CORPORAL STODDART (*going up R and looking out of the window, back*) Christ, there's another of our men 'it by the blarsted sniper! 'E's knocking abaht 'ere somewheres. (*Venomously*) Gord, wen we gets the blighter, we'll give 'im the cold steel, we will. We'll jab the belly aht of 'im, we will!

(*MRS GOGAN enters tearfully by the door R; she is a little proud of the importance of being connected with death*)

MRS GOGAN (*to Fluther*) I'll never forget what you done for me, Fluther, goin' around at th' risk of your life settlin' everything with th' undhertaker an' th' cemetery people. When all me own were afraid to put their noses out, you plunged like a good one through hummin' bullets, an' they knockin' fire out o' th' road, tinklin' through th' frightened windows, an' splashin' themselves to pieces on th' walls! An' you'll find, that Mollser in th' happy place she's gone to, won't forget to whisper, now an' again, th' name o' Fluther.

(CORPORAL STODDART *comes from the window down* R *to the door* R, *and stands near the door*)

CORPORAL STODDART (*to Mrs Gogan*) Git it aht, mother, git it aht.

BESSIE (*from the chair*) It's excusin' me you'll be, Mrs Gogan, for not stannin' up, seein' I'm shaky on me feet for want of a little sleep, an' not desirin' to show any disrespect to poor little Mollser.

FLUTHER. Sure, we all know, Bessie, that it's vice versa with you.

MRS GOGAN (*to Bessie*) Indeed, it's meself that has well chronicled, Mrs Burgess, all your gentle hurryin's to me little Mollser, when she was alive, bringin' her somethin' to dhrink, or somethin' t'eat, an' never passin' her without lifting up her heart with a delicate word o' kindness.

CORPORAL STODDART (*impatiently, but kindly*) Git it aht, git it aht, mother.

(*The men rise from their card-playing;* FLUTHER *and* BRENNAN *go* R *to the* R *end of the coffin;* PETER *and* COVEY *go* L *of the table to the* L *end of the coffin. One of them takes the box and candles out of the way. They carry the coffin down* R *and out by the door* R, CORPORAL STODDART *watching them.* MRS GOGAN *follows the coffin out.*

There is a pause. CORPORAL STODDART, *at the door* R, *turns towards Bessie*)

(*To Bessie, who is almost asleep*) 'Ow many men is in this 'ere 'ouse? (*No answer. Loudly*) 'Ow many men is in this 'ere 'ouse?

BESSIE (*waking with a start*) God, I was nearly asleep! . . . How many men? Didn't you see them?

CORPORAL STODDART. Are they all that are in the 'ouse?

BESSIE (*sleepily*) Oh, there's none higher up, but there may be more lower down. Why?

CORPORAL STODDART. All men in the district 'as to be rounded up. Somebody's giving 'elp to the snipers, an' we 'as to tike precautions. If I 'ad my wy I'd mike 'em all join up an' do their bit! But I suppose they an' you are all Shinners.

BESSIE (*who has been sinking into sleep, waking up to a sleepy vehemence*) Bessie Burgess is no Shinner, an' never had no thruck with anything spotted be th' fingers o' th' Fenians. But always made it her business to harness herself for Church whenever she knew that God Save The King was goin' to be sung at t'end of th' service; whose only son went to th' front in th' first contingent of the Dublin Fusiliers, an' that's on his way home carryin' a shatthered arm that he got fightin' for his King an' counthry!

(BESSIE'S *head sinks slowly forward again. The door* R *opens and* PETER *comes in, his body stiff, and his face contorted with anger. He goes up* R, *to the back, and paces angrily from side to side.* COVEY, *with a sly grin on his face, and* FLUTHER *follow Peter.* FLUTHER *goes to* L *and* COVEY *goes to* R *end of the table.* BRENNAN *follows in and slinks*

to back of the table to the L *corner between the dresser and the door* L.
CORPORAL STODDART *remains standing a little in from the door* R)

FLUTHER (*after an embarrassing pause*) Th' air in th' sthreet outside's shakin' with the firin' o' rifles, an' machine-guns. It must be a hot shop in th' middle o' th' scrap.
CORPORAL STODDART. We're pumping lead in on 'em from every side, now; they'll soon be shoving up th' white flag.
PETER (*with a shout at Fluther and Covey*) I'm tellin' you either o' yous two lowsers 'ud make a betther hearseman than Peter! proddin' an' pokin' at me an' I helpin' to carry out a corpse!
FLUTHER (*provokingly*) It wasn't a very derogatory thing for th' Covey to say that you'd make a fancy hearseman, was it?
PETER (*furiously*) A pair o' redjesthered bowseys pondherin' from mornin' till night on how they'll get a chance to break a gap through th' quiet nature of a man that's always endeavourin' to chase out of him any sthray thought of venom against his fella-man!
THE COVEY. Oh, shut it, shut it, shut it!
PETER (*furiously*) As long as I'm a livin' man, responsible for me thoughts, words an' deeds to th' Man above, I'll feel meself instituted to fight again' th' sliddherin' ways of a pair o' picaroons, whisperin', concurrin', concoctin', an' conspirin' together to rendher me unconscious of th' life I'm thryin' to live!
CORPORAL STODDART (*dumbfounded*) What's wrong, Paddy; wot 'ave they done to you?
PETER (*savagely to the Corporal*) You mind your own business! What's it got to do with you, what's wrong with me?
BESSIE (*in a sleepy murmur*) Will yous thry to conthrol yourselves into quietness? Yous'll waken her . . . up . . . on . . . me . . . again. (*She sleeps*)
FLUTHER (*coming* C) Come on, boys, to th' cards again, an' never mind him.
CORPORAL STODDART. No use of you going to start cards; you'll be going aht of 'ere, soon as Sergeant comes.
FLUTHER (*in surprise*) Goin' out o' here? An' why're we goin' out o' here?
CORPORAL STODDART. All men in district 'as to be rounded up, an' 'eld in till the scrap is over.
FLUTHER (*concerned*) An' where're we goin' to be held in?
CORPORAL STODDART. They're puttin' them in a church.
COVEY (*astounded*) A church?
FLUTHER. What sort of a church? Is it a Protestan' church?
CORPORAL STODDART. I dunno; I suppose so.
FLUTHER (*in dismay*) Be God, it'll be a nice thing to be stuck all night in a Protestan' church!
CORPORAL STODDART. If I was you, I'd bring the cards—you might get a chance of a gime.

FLUTHER (*hesitant*) Ah, no, that wouldn't do . . . I wondher . . . (*After a moment's thought*) Ah, I don't think we'd be doin' anything derogatory be playin' cards in a Protestan' church.

CORPORAL STODDART. If I was you I'd bring a little snack with me; you might be glad of it before the morning. (*Lilting*) Oh, I do like a snice mince pie,
Oh, I do like a snice mince pie.

(*Again the snap of the sniper's rifle rings out, followed by a scream of pain.* CORPORAL STODDART *goes pale, runs up* R *to near the window* C, *with his rifle at the ready*)

VOICES (*in the street to* R, *chanting*) Red Cr . . . oss . . . Red Cr . . . oss! Ambu . . . lance . . . Ambu . . . lance!

(*The door* R *is dashed open, and* SERGEANT TINLEY, *pale, agitated, and angry, comes rapidly in. He stands inside the door, glaring at the men in the room.* CORPORAL STODDART *swings round at the ready as Tinley enters and lets his rifle drop when he sees the Sergeant*)

CORPORAL STODDART (*to the Sergeant*) One of our men 'it again, Sergeant?

SERGEANT TINLEY (*angrily*) Private Taylor: got it right through the chest, 'e did; an 'ole in front as ow you could put your 'and through, an' arf 'is back blown awy! Dum-dum bullets they're using. Gang of assassins potting at us from behind roofs. That's not plying the gime: why won't they come into the open and fight fair?

FLUTHER (*unable to stand the slight, facing the Sergeant*) Fight fair! A few hundhred scrawls o' chaps with a couple o' guns an' Rosary beads, again' a hundhred thousand thrained men with horse, fut an' artillery . . . (*To the others in the room*) An' he wants us to fight fair! (*To the Sergeant*) D'ye want us to come out in our skins an' throw stones?

SERGEANT TINLEY (*to the Corporal*) Are these four all that are 'ere?

CORPORAL STODDART. Four; that's hall, Sergeant.

SERGEANT TINLEY (*roughly*) Come on, then, get the blighters aht. (*To the men*) 'Ere, 'op it aht! Aht into the street with you, an' if another of our men goes west, you go with 'im. (*He catches Fluther by the arm*) Go on, git aht!

FLUTHER (*pulling himself free*) Eh, who are you chuckin', eh?

SERGEANT TINLEY (*roughly*) Go on, git aht, you blighter.

FLUTHER (*truculently*) Who're you callin' a blighter to, eh? I'm a Dublin man, born an' bred in th' City, see?

SERGEANT TINLEY. Oh, I don't care if you were Bryan Buroo; git aht, git aht.

FLUTHER (*pausing as he reaches the door* R, *to face the Sergeant defiantly*) Jasus, you an' your guns! Leave them down, an' I'd beat th' two of yous without sweatin'!

(*Shepherded by the two soldiers, who follow them out,* PETER, COVEY, FLUTHER *and* BRENNAN *go out by the door* R.
BESSIE *is sleeping heavily on the chair by the fire. After a pause* NORA *appears at the door* L, *in her nightdress. Remaining at the door for a few moments she looks vaguely around the room. She then comes in quietly, goes over to the fire, pokes it and puts the kettle on. She thinks for a few moments, pressing her hand to her forehead. She looks questioningly at the fire, and then at the press at back. She goes to the dresser* L, *back, opens a drawer, takes out a soiled cloth and spreads it on the table. She then places things for tea on the table*)

NORA. I imagine th' room looks very odd, somehow . . . I was nearly forgetting Jack's tea . . . Ah, I think I'll have everything done before he gets in . . . (*She lilts gently, as she arranges the table*)
Th' violets were scenting th' woods, Nora,
          Displaying their charms to th' bee,
    When I first said I lov'd only you, Nora,
          An' you said you lov'd only me.

    Th' chestnut blooms gleam'd through th' glade, Nora,
          A robin sang loud from a tree,
    When I first said I lov'd only you, Nora,
          An' you said you lov'd only me.

(*She pauses suddenly, and glances round the room. Doubtfully*) I can't help feelin' this room very strange . . . What is it? . . . What is it? . . . I must think . . . I must thry to remember . . .
VOICES (*chanting in a distant street*) Ambu . . . lance, Ambu . . . lance! Red Cro . . . ss, Red Cro . . . ss!
NORA (*startled and listening for a moment, then resuming the arrangement of the table*) Trees, birds an' bees sang a song, Nora,
          Of happier transports to be,
    When I first said I lov'd only you, Nora,
          An' you said you lov'd only me.

(*A burst of rifle-fire is heard in a street near by, followed by the rapid tok-tok-tok of a machine-gun*)
(*Staring in front of her and screaming*) Jack, Jack, Jack! My baby, my baby, my baby!
BESSIE (*waking with a start*) You divil, are you afther gettin' out o' bed again!

(BESSIE *rises and runs towards* NORA, *who rushes to the window, back* L *which she frantically opens*)

NORA (*at the window, screaming*) Jack, Jack, for God's sake, come to me!
SOLDIERS (*outside, shouting*) Git awoy, git awoy from that window, there!

BESSIE (*seizing hold of Nora*) Come away, come away, woman from that window!

NORA (*struggling with Bessie*) Where is it; where have you hidden it? Oh, Jack, Jack, where are you?

BESSIE (*imploringly*) Mrs Clitheroe, for God's sake, come away!

NORA (*fiercely*) I won't; he's below. Let . . . me . . . go! You're thryin' to keep me from me husband. I'll follow him. Jack, Jack, come to your Nora!

BESSIE. Hus-s-sh, Nora! He'll be here in a minute. I'll bring him to you, if you'll only be quiet—honest to God, I will.

(*With a great effort* BESSIE *pushes Nora away from the window, the force used causes her to stagger against it herself. Two rifle-shots ring out in quick succession.* BESSIE *jerks her body convulsively; stands stiffly upright for a moment, a look of agonized astonishment on her face, then she staggers forward, leaning heavily on the table with her hands*)

(*With an arrested scream of fear and pain*) Merciful God, I'm shot, I'm shot, I'm shot! . . . Th' life's pourin' out o' me! (*To Nora*) I've got this through . . . through you . . . through you, you bitch, you! . . . O God, have mercy on me! . . . (*To Nora*) You wouldn't stop quiet, no you wouldn't, you wouldn't, blast you! Look at what I'm after gettin', look at what I'm after gettin' . . . I'm bleedin' to death, an' no one's here to stop th' flowin' blood! (*Calling*) Mrs Gogan, Mrs Gogan! Fluther, Fluther, for God's sake, somebody, a doctor, a doctor!

(BESSIE, *leaving the* R *end of the table, staggers down towards the door* R, *but, weakening, she sinks down on her knees,* RC, *then reclining, she supports herself by her right hand resting on the floor.* NORA *is rigid with her back to the wall* L, *her trembling hands held out a little from her sides; her lips quivering, her breast heaving, staring wildly at the figure of Bessie*)

NORA (*in a breathless whisper*) Jack, I'm frightened . . . I'm frightened, Jack . . . Oh, Jack, where are you?

BESSIE (*moaningly*) This is what's after comin' on me for nursin' you day an' night . . . I was a fool, a fool, a fool! Get me a dhrink o' wather, you jade, will you? There's a fire burnin' in me blood! (*Pleadingly*) Nora, Nora, dear, for God's sake, run out an' get Mrs Gogan, or Fluther, or somebody to bring a doctor, quick, quick, quick! (*As Nora does not stir*) Blast you, stir yourself, before I'm gone!

NORA. Oh, Jack, Jack, where are you?

BESSIE (*in a whispered moan*) Jesus Christ, me sight's goin'! It's all dark, dark! Nora, hold me hand!

(BESSIE'S *body lists over and she sinks into a prostrate position on the floor*)

I'm dyin', I'm dyin' . . . I feel it . . . Oh God, oh God! (*She feebly sings*) I do believe . . . I will believe
      That . . . Jesus . . . died . . . for . . . me,
      That . . . on . . . the . . . cross He . . . shed . . . His . . . blood
      From . . . sin . . . to . . . set . . . free.

      (BESSIE *ceases singing, and lies stretched out, still and rigid. There is a pause; then* MRS GOGAN *runs hastily in by the door* R. *She halts at the door and looks round with a frightened air*)

      MRS GOGAN (*quivering with fear*) Blessed be God, what's afther happenin! (*To Nora*) What's wrong, child, what's wrong? (*She sees Bessie, runs to her and bends over the body*) Bessie, Bessie! (*She shakes the body*) Mrs Burgess, Mrs Burgess! (*She feels Bessie's forehead*) My God, she's as cold as death. They're afther murdherin' th' poor inoffensive woman!

      (SERGEANT TINLEY *and* CORPORAL STODDART, *in agitation, enter by the door* R, *their rifles at the ready*)

      SERGEANT TINLEY (*excitedly*) This is the 'ouse! (*They go rapidly to the window, back* C) That's the window!

      NORA (*pressing back against the wall*) Hide it, hide it; cover it up, cover it up!

      (SERGEANT TINLEY, *looking round the room, sees the body. He comes from the window to Bessie, and bends over her*)

      SERGEANT TINLEY (*bending over the body*) 'Ere, wot's this? Oo's this? Oh, God, we've plugged one of the women of the 'ouse!

      CORPORAL STODDART (*at the window*) W'y the 'ell did she go to the window? Is she dead?

      SERGEANT TINLEY. Dead as bedamned. Well, we couldn't afford to tike any chances.

      (SERGEANT TINLEY *goes back to the window, and looks out*)

      NORA (*screaming, and putting her hands before her face*) Hide it, hide it; don't let me see it! Take me away, take me away, Mrs Gogan!

      (MRS GOGAN, *who has been weeping softly over Bessie, rises, and crosses by the front of the table to the room* L, *goes in and comes out with a sheet in her hands. She crosses over and spreads the sheet over Bessie's body*)

      MRS GOGAN (*as she spreads the sheet*) Oh, God help her, th' poor woman, she's stiffenin' out as hard as she can! Her face has written on it th' shock o' sudden agony, an' her hands is whitenin' into th' smooth shininess of wax.

      NORA (*whimperingly*) Take me away, take me away; don't leave me here to be lookin' an' lookin' at it!

      MRS GOGAN (*going over to Nora and putting her arm round her*) Come on with me, dear, an' you can doss in poor Mollser's bed, till we gather some neighbours to come an' give th' last friendly touches to Bessie in th' lonely layin' of her out.

(MRS GOGAN *puts her arms round* NORA, *leads her across from* L *to* R, *and they both go slowly out by the door* R.

CORPORAL STODDART *comes from the window to the table, looks at the tea-things on the table; goes to the fireplace, and takes the teapot up in his hand*)

CORPORAL STODDART (*over to Tinley, at the window*) Tea here, Sergeant; wot abaht a cup of scald?

SERGEANT TINLEY. Pour it aht, pour it aht, Stoddart—I could scoff anything just now.

(CORPORAL STODDART *pours out two cups of tea.* SERGEANT TINLEY *comes from the window to the table, and sits on the* R *end;* CORPORAL STODDART *sits on the opposite end of the table, and they drink the tea. In the distance is heard a bitter burst of rifle and machine-gun fire, interspersed with the boom, boom of artillery. The glare in the sky seen through the window* C, *back, flares into a fuller and a deeper red*)

SERGEANT TINLEY. There gows the general attack on the Powst Office.

VOICES (*in a distant street*) Ambu . . . lance, Ambu . . . lance! Red Cro . . . ss, Red Cro . . . ss!

(*The voices of soldiers at a barricade outside the house are heard singing*)

> They were summoned from the 'illside,
> They were called in from the glen,
> And the country found 'em ready
> At the stirring call for men.
> Let not tears add to their 'ardship,
> As the soldiers pass along,
> And although our 'eart is breaking,
> Make it sing this cheery song.

(SERGEANT TINLEY *and* CORPORAL STODDART *join in the chorus as they sip the tea*)

SERGEANT TINLEY *and* CORPORAL STODDART (*singing*) Keep the
> 'ome fires burning,
> While your 'earts are yearning,
> Though your lads are far away,
> They dream of 'ome;
> There's a silver lining
> Through the dark cloud shining,
> Turn the dark cloud inside out,
> Till the boys come 'ome!

CURTAIN

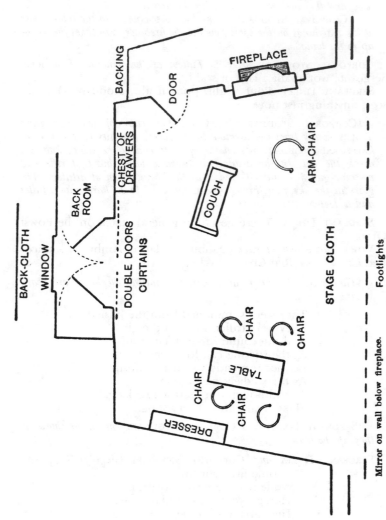

PROPERTY AND FURNITURE PLOT

ACT I

Curtains for door to room, back, and for window, room, back
Chest of drawers
Dresser
Table and four or five chairs. Cloth for table
Couch
Clock, small wall mirror
Green bowl, filled with flowers
Pictures of 'The Angelus', and 'The Gleaners'
Picture of 'The Sleeping Venus'
Linoleum for floor
Hat, in cardboard box
Claw hammer, turnscrew, white apron, rule for FLUTHER
Bright green cut-a-way coat, with gold braid, sword
Black, broad-brimmed hat with white plume, white cord breeches, top boots,
    white frilled shirt for PETER
Folded linen in chest of drawers
Clothes brush in drawer of chest of drawers
Suit of dungarees, red tie and book for COVEY
Handbill for FLUTHER
Stiff collar for PETER
Sam Browne belt, revolver with holster for CLITHEROE
Sam Browne belt, revolver with holster, dark green tweed uniform, slouch hat,
    caught up one side with a small red hand badge, for BRENNAN
Green-grey uniform with green-grey puttees, cap with peak, Sam Browne belt,
    revolver and holster for LANGON
Cigarettes for CLITHEROE
Teapot in fireplace

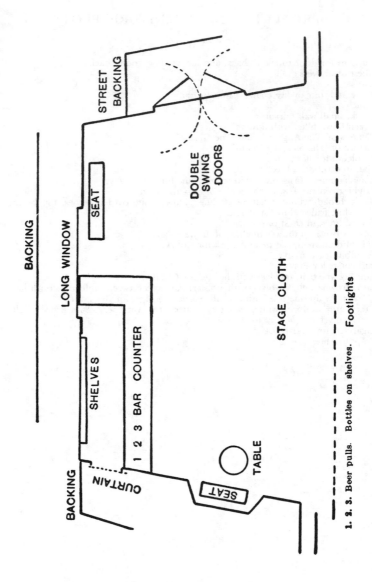

STREET BACKING

DOUBLE SWING DOORS

BACKING

LONG WINDOW

SEAT

STAGE CLOTH

SHELVES

1 2 3 BAR COUNTER

BACKING

CURTAIN

SEAT

TABLE

1. 2. 3. Beer pulls.   Bottles on shelves.   Footlights

ACT II

Counter with beer-pulls. Shelves behind counter with bottles
Two seats
Round table
Coloured show cards
Glasses and carafe of water
Shawls for BESSIE and ROSIE
Ornament for ROSIE's hair
Coins for FLUTHER, COVEY and CLITHEROE
Plough and Stars banner for BRENNAN; green, white and yellow Tricolour for
     LANGON
Baby for MRS GOGAN

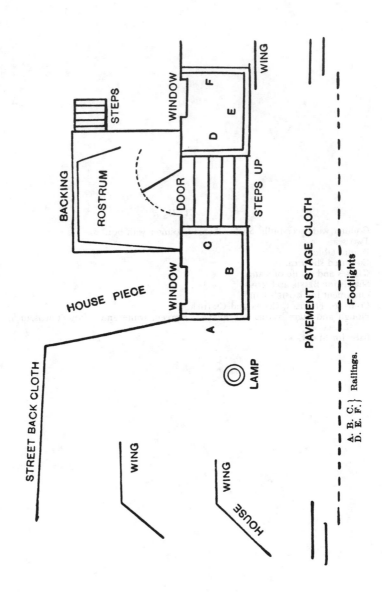

ACT III

A street lamp
Kitchen chair
Perambulator
Standard lamp with bright-coloured shade
A few red, green, or yellow evening-dresses
Some boxes of shoes
Neck fur, umbrellas, box of biscuits for BESSIE
Two worn coins and short, narrow strip of wood or tin for the COVEY
Gaudily trimmed woman's hat, tunic shirt and jar of whiskey for FLUTHER
Mug of milk for BESSIE
Spectacles for PETER
Mackintosh for NORA
Sack of flour for the COVEY
Rifle for CLITHEROE
See sketch of scene

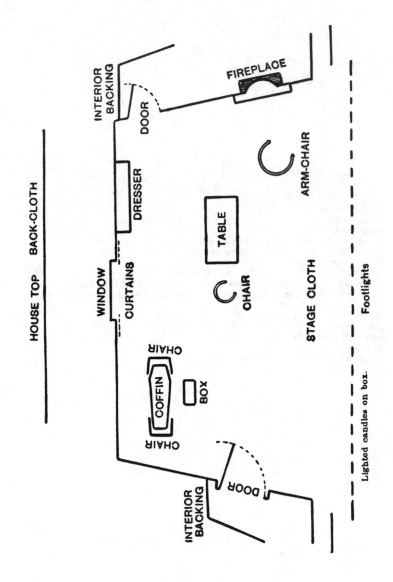

ACT IV

Old dresser with Delft and materials for tea-making
A coffin
Two candles in candlesticks
A box
Small kitchen table, and three kitchen chairs
Old armchair
Kettle and teapot in fireplace
Nightdress and slippers for NORA
Pack of cards
Bottle of whiskey for FLUTHER
Uniforms, tin helmets, and rifles for British soldiers
Coat with holes for BRENNAN
Soiled tablecloth
Sheet for MRS GOGAN

LIGHTING PLOT

ACT I

White strip at door R
Fire on
Floats and No. 1 batten, two-thirds up, ambers. Come up to full when NORA brings in lighted lamp

ACT II

Two deep-blue floods on cloth at large window, back
Floats (white) and No. 1 batten, full up. No changes

ACT III

Floats (white) and full up, also Nos. 1 and 2 battens
Two white floats off R, at upper entrance of lane
Start check down by one-third at FLUTHER'S entrance with whiskey-jar; completed as FLUTHER is pulled into house

ACT IV

Amber foots and No. 1 batten, half up
Fire on
Two amber strips on door L
No strip on door R
Two special red floods on illuminated cloth at window, back; these to be on dimmers, so that red glow rises and falls during Act, to indicate fires in city

NOTES

Pictures other than 'The Gleaners', or 'The Angelus' would do.

Peter's coat is a cut-a-way, of the pattern worn in 1800; it is of a bright green, with gold braid on shoulders and wrists. It is supposed to be a replica of the costume worn by Robert Emmett, the Irish Patriot, executed in 1803. The Irish National Foresters is merely a benevolent Society, and those who wear the costume worn by Peter are a subject of amusement to intelligent Irishmen.

The banner of 'The Plough and the Stars' was the banner of the Irish Citizen Army, and was blue, bearing on the field a plough, with the starry constellation added. The Tricolour was the banner of the Irish Republicans —since adopted by the Irish Government—and consisted of three vertical stripes of green, white and orange (yellow). The Insurrection of 1916 was carried out by the military section of the Irish Labour Movement, the Irish Citizen Army, and by the secret organization known as the Irish Republican Brotherhood.

In the play the banner of 'The Plough and the Stars', which is not displayed, may be simply a banner of blue.

The railing round the house, and the steps up to door of the house, in the third act, may, if means do not allow, be left out. The street lamp may also be omitted.

Printed in Great Britain by
Redwood Books, Trowbridge, Wiltshire